Public sector reform needs to move on from the narrow agenda of New Public Management, and this includes treating the question of public service 'ethics' as something more substantial than rhetoric. The authors of this important book provide substantial ideas and material that will be of value to those involved in that task.

Colin Crouch, *Professor Emeritus,*
University of Warwick, UK

This accessible text is firmly grounded in ethical theory and current public management practice. Well chosen case vignettes allow the reader to apply principles and consider their universality. The inclusion of ethical dimensions of the delivery of public services through networks also makes this text relevant to private and voluntary sector audiences.

Dr Gemma Donnelly-Cox, *School of Business,*
Trinity College Dublin

This is a timely contribution to highlight the complex nature of ethical practice. It succeeds in reminding us that ethics always is at play, wittingly or unwittingly. It is a welcome invitation to think of responsibility through the lens of both personal and organisational ethics that can support sustainable action in public management.

Dr Manuela Nocker, *Senior Lecturer in Organisation Studies and*
Innovation, Essex University Business School, UK

D0303368

Ethics and Management in the Public Sector

Grappling with ethical issues is a daily challenge for those working in organizations that deliver public services. Such services are delivered through an often bewildering range of agencies, and amidst this constant change there are fears that a public service ethos, a tradition of working in the public interest, becomes blurred.

Using extensive vignettes and case studies, *Ethics and Management in the Public Sector* illuminates the practical decisions made by public officials. The book takes a universal approach to ethics, reflecting the worldwide impact of public service reforms. This textbook covers important themes reflecting current thinking, including an examination of:

- the definition and scope of ethical issues for public service organizations
- the universality of ethical principles and the relativity of values
- the extent to which Western ethical principles are appropriate in other parts of the world
- the impact of reforms on traditional values and principles of public service.

This easy-to-use textbook is a definitive guide for postgraduate students of public sector ethics, as well as students of public management and administration more generally.

Alan Lawton is currently Deputy Head of the School of Business and Economics, Monash University, Gippsland, Australia. He has written extensively on public sector management and public sector ethics. He has advised governments on codes of conduct for public officials and worked with a range of government organizations on ethics training.

Julie Rayner is Lecturer in the School of Business and Economics at Monash University, Gippsland, Australia. Prior to joining Monash, Julie taught at Durham University, UK and also worked with The Open University Business School. Her research interests are in public sector organizations and she has recently published in the *Journal of Public Administration Research and Theory, Journal of Business Ethics* and the *International Journal of Human Resource Management*.

Karin Lasthuizen is Associate Professor in Governance Studies and senior member of the research group Quality of Governance at the Department of Governance Studies at the VU University in Amsterdam, the Netherlands. She has recently published in the *Public Management Review, Public Administration, Sociological Methods and Research* and the *International Journal of Leadership*.

ROUTLEDGE MASTERS IN PUBLIC MANAGEMENT

Edited by Stephen P. Osborne, Owen Hughes and Walter Kickert

Routledge Masters in Public Management series is an integrated set of texts. It is intended to form the backbone for the holistic study of the theory and practice of public management as part of

- a taught Masters, MBA or MPA course at a university or college
- a work-based, in-service programme of education and training, or
- a programme of self-guided study.

Each volume stands alone in its treatment of its topic, whether it be strategic management, marketing or procurement and is co-authored by leading specialists in their field. However, all volumes in the series share both a common pedagogy and a common approach to the structure of the text. Key features of all volumes in the series include:

- a critical approach to combining theory with practice which educates its reader, rather than solely teaching him/her a set of skills
- clear learning objectives for each chapter
- the use of figures, tables and boxes to highlight key ideas, concepts and skills
- an annotated bibliography, guiding students in their further reading, and
- a dedicated case study in the topic of each volume, to serve as a focus for discussion and learning.

Managing Change and Innovation in
Public Service Organizations
Stephen P. Osborne and Kerry Brown

Risk and Crisis Management in the
Public Sector
Lynn T. Drennan and Allan McConnell

Contracting for Public Services
Carsten Greve

Performance Management in the
Public Sector
*Wouter van Dooren, Geert Bouckaert
and John Halligan*

Financial Management and
Accounting in the Public Sector
Gary Bandy

Strategic Leadership in the Public
Sector
Paul Joyce

Managing Local Governments:
Designing Management Control
Systems that Deliver Value
*Emanuele Padovani and David W.
Young*

Marketing Management and
Communications in the Public Sector
*Martial Pasquier and Jean-Patrick
Villeneuve*

Ethics and Management in the Public
Sector
*Alan Lawton, Julie Rayner and
Karin Lasthuizen*

Ethics and Management in the Public Sector

Alan Lawton,
Julie Rayner and
Karin Lasthuizen

 Routledge
Taylor & Francis Group

LONDON AND NEW YORK

First published 2013
by Routledge
2 Park Square, Milton Park, Abingdon, Oxon OX14 4RN

Simultaneously published in the USA and Canada
by Routledge
711 Third Avenue, New York, NY 10017

Routledge is an imprint of the Taylor & Francis Group, an informa business

British Library Cataloguing in Publication Data
A catalogue record for this book is available from the British Library

Library of Congress Cataloging in Publication Data
Lawton, Alan.
  Ethics and management in the public sector/Alan Lawton,
  Karin Lasthuizen and Julie Rayner.
    p. cm. -- (Routledge masters in public management)
  Includes bibliographical references and index.
  1. Public administration—Moral and ethical aspects. 2. Civil
  service ethics. I. Lasthuizen, Karin. II. Rayner, Julie, 1961–
  III. Title.
  JF1525.E8L38 2012
  172'.2—dc23   2012017989

ISBN: 978-0-415-57759-5(hbk)
ISBN: 978-0-415-57760-1 (pbk)
ISBN: 978-0-203-09412-9 (ebk)

Typeset in Bembo and Bell Gothic
by Florence Production Ltd, Stoodleigh, Devon, UK

We dedicate this book to the memory of
Jolanta Palidauskaite, colleague and friend.

Contents

Illustrations

FIGURES

TABLES

EXERCISES

BOXES

Acknowledgements

We would like to acknowledge the contributions made to the development of ideas expressed in this book, particularly in Chapters 3, 6, 8 and 9 by Michael Macaulay, Frederique Six and Leone Heres. We would also like to thank Annemarie Mastenbroek for her comments throughout.

Chapter 1

Managing ethics in the public services

LEARNING OBJECTIVES

By the end of this chapter you should:

- be clear about the overall structure of the book
- understand why ethics is important for public service organizations and the individuals who work in and for them
- understand what it is that makes an issue an ethical issue as distinct from, say, a legal or a political issue
- have a sense of the scope of ethical decisions.

KEY POINTS IN THIS CHAPTER

- Ethics is an integral part of the public services and is not a 'left-over' to be considered after other issues have been taken into account.
- Ethics is not just about resolving dilemmas.

KEY TERMS

- **Public officials** – defined generically to include elected politicians, appointed administrators and managers, and professionals who deliver public services such as social workers, teachers, doctors and nurses, the police, fire-fighters and so on.
- **Ethical issues** – those issues, distinct from political, legal or social, that are concerned with right and wrong actions and outcomes for both individuals and the organizations they work for.

■ **Ethics** is defined as a set of principles that provide a framework for right action; an individual acts in accordance with that set of principles.

WHY SHOULD WE BE CONCERNED WITH ETHICS?

This might seem a trite question. 'Of course we should be concerned with ethics' you might respond. However, it seems to us that if this was so obvious, why is it that we read in the newspapers every day about a corrupt public official in this part of the world, or a rigged election in that part of the world? As much as we might like to think that such things never happen in our own countries, they do and will continue to do so. Two of the authors of this book have lived in the UK, a country that generally has a reputation for being relatively 'clean' and where corrupt behaviour on the part of public officials is considered to be the rare exception rather than the rule. And yet, during 2009–10, there was revelation after revelation concerning Members of Parliament fiddling their expenses, as part of a self-determined and self-policed expenses regime (see Kelly 2009). The integrity of MPs plummeted to an all-time low. As a result, a new Independent Parliamentary Standards Authority was added to the already existing committees and agencies that have some responsibility for dealing with standards of conduct of public officials both appointed and elected. It appears to be no longer the case that we can rely on the personal integrity of officials to act according to ethical norms and we need to put in place compliance mechanisms to patrol the behaviour of individuals. We examine the balance between a compliance approach and an integrity approach to ethics in Chapters 6 and 7.

Not that there is anything new about such revelations. In the UK, recent history has seen numerous examples of unethical behaviour from the scandals involving property development and local authority contracting in the 1960s, the so-called Poulson Affair (see Doig 1984) to more recent concerns with 'cash for questions' that hastened the end of the Conservative government in 1997 and led to the creation of the Committee on Standards in Public Life and the drafting of the Principles of Public Life, the so-called Nolan Principles. In Queensland, Australia, the Fitzgerald inquiry into political and police corruption (1987–9) precipitated the collapse of the Joh Bjelke-Petersen government and in Hong Kong the Independent Commission Against Corruption (ICAC) was created in 1974 to clean up endemic corruption in government and the police force. We can reach back in time and across continents to find examples of unethical and corrupt behaviour. A key question then becomes, to what extent is human nature corrupt or corruptible? Will there always be such examples or is there something in cultures – social, organizational, national or ethnic – that condones or encourages corrupt behaviour? We address this question in Chapter 5.

Of course, public sector organizations are not the only places where corrupt behaviour is found. You will, no doubt, be familiar with examples of corrupt behaviour in the private sector (such as Enron), and ongoing investigations into multinationals (such as BAE) for bribery and corruption in the armaments industry. At the time of writing this chapter, headlines in the morning papers report on four executives of the Anglo-Australian mining company Rio Tinto being found guilty in China of bribery charges. The firm's Chief Executive, Tom Albanese, commented: 'Ethical behaviour is at the heart of everything we do' (Branigan 2010). No doubt you can provide your own examples. What is of particular interest for the purposes of this book is, first, how international agencies such as the World Bank, the Organisation for Economic Co-operation and Development (OECD) or the United Nations have responded to what appears to be the globalization of ethical issues. Second, as public service organizations are encouraged to be more 'business-like' in the way they operate, to what extent have they become 'corrupted', as some critics claim, by engagement with the private sector?

WHAT MAKES AN ISSUE AN ETHICAL ISSUE?

It is not always clear as to what constitutes unethical behaviour as distinct from illegal or inappropriate behaviour. Indeed there is frequent overlap as ethical issues are often regulated through legislation, and what counts as unethical behaviour may vary from culture to culture and country to country. We know there is a grey area in, say, at which point a gift becomes a bribe. We might focus upon the act itself – what is done: examples might include fraud and corruption. Such acts are often legislated for and are clearly defined. Other acts, such as bullying or harassment, are, perhaps, less clear-cut. Huberts, Pijl, and Steen (1999) use a taxonomy of integrity violations as the basis for their research and these include corruption, fraud, theft, conflicts of interest, improper use of authority, manipulation and misuse of information, discrimination, sexual harassment and bullying, waste and abuse, and private time misconduct.

Apart from what is done we might be interested in how it is done. For example, how do public officials treat their patients, students or clients in terms of duty, obligations, care, equality and so on? It seems to us that much of the public services are about the quality of the relationships that are built up between citizens and the State, in all its forms. We might also be interested in who defines acceptable behaviour in the first place. Is it written down as a code of conduct, both for society as a whole in terms of a religious document, or for the organization in terms of a rule book? Is good conduct defined by a religious leader, a chief executive or by individual conscience? To what extent do individuals leave their personal values at the door when they enter organizational life and are they, as it were, 'blank sheets' upon which the organization can write its own values – ethical or otherwise – onto its employees? We explore these issues in Chapters 2 and 3.

One immediate issue that is raised is the extent to which there is agreement in a set of universal ethics. We have already introduced the question of when does a gift become a bribe; this simple question raises all kinds of complex issues of cultural relativity. The position we take in this book is that there are common problems that are given specific meanings locally. Thus, we might all recognize that injustice or inequality occurs in a given situation, but they may take different local forms. One simple manifestation of this was brought home to one of the authors when developing codes of conduct for government ministers, MPs, civil servants and judges in Ethiopia. Most codes of conduct will include a register of interests, either as an integral part of the code or as a separate document. Such a register of interests is to ensure transparency, particularly where there may be possible conflicts of interest. Those who are subject to the register, the registree, usually have to include members of their family so that, for example, family members do not benefit from the position or post of the registree. The problem arises when defining the family. In a Western context this might mean the partner and children of the registree and those who live in the same household. In other parts of the world the concept of the family is not only extended, but it is expected that the head of the family will seek to favour those extended members. Is this unethical? We will return to this question later.

We might also wonder if ethical issues are the same throughout the organization. Public service organizations tend to be large and provide a number of different functions. A local municipality might be responsible for education, social care, the environment, housing, local roads, refuse collection and so on. It may also provide 'back-office' services including payroll, human resources, audit and corporate strategy. It may also be run by politicians (local or national), administrators, professionals or a combination of all of these. It would be unrealistic, therefore, to expect one homogeneous culture or set of values to be applied across the organization as a whole. Public service organizations are typically dynamic, complex and consist of competing values and sub-cultures. Individuals working within these organizations will have to manage a complex set of relationships and values as they are subject to departmental norms, professional values, organizational rules plus the needs of their clients or users, let alone their own individual conscience.

The simple exercise below (Exercise 1.1) is a useful ice-breaker for opening up a discussion of what constitutes an ethical issue.

We have used this simple exercise on many occasions and the most interesting discussions are around the 'Depends' response. How large or small is the gift? How restrictive are the rules? What were the implications of a colleague's mistake? Rarely is it possible to answer with a straight YES or NO.

THE CONTEXT OF ETHICS

Private sector organizations are often considered to be more dynamic, pay more, offer more interesting work, provide quicker career progression and so on. In contrast public service organizations are often characterized as slow-moving bureaucracies, bound by red tape, dominated by rules and slow to innovate. So why do

EXERCISE 1.1 PRACTICES

In an organization do you think that the following constitute unethical practices?

	YES	NO	DEPENDS	DON'T KNOW
1. Covering up for a colleague's mistakes				
2. Acting in favour of a client/customer out of friendship				
3. Acting in favour of a client for a bribe				
4. Recruiting/promoting staff on the basis of family ties or friendship				
5. Accepting corporate hospitality such as tickets to a sporting event				
6. Discriminating against staff on the basis of age, religion, gender, colour, etc.				
7. Presenting misleading information				
8. Manipulating performance figures to meet targets				
9. Using office equipment for personal use				
10. Rewarding people differently				
11. Telling small lies to clients such as 'your case is now at the top of the list'				
12. Blaming others for your mistakes				
13. Bending the rules to help the organization				
14. Bending the rules to help clients, patients or students				
15. Using the organization's phone for personal communications				
16. Using the internet or social media sites during office time				
17. Using the internet during office time to order goods and services				
18. Taking longer than necessary to do a job				

individuals work in the public services? Sometimes, the public sector is the only game in town and individuals have no alternatives but to join the local municipality or government office. And yet, there is a wealth of research that confirms the existence of a public service ethos and that individuals are motivated by this ethos. We look at this in more detail in Chapter 4. For the moment, let us accept that there is a public service ethos and that individuals are motivated to act in the public interest, howsoever defined. Those that work in, and for, the public services are said to put public interests before their own private interests. There is a set of principles that govern the behaviour of these individuals and form the context for their behaviour. We feel let down when our public officials act in breach of these principles. Many countries have put in place regulatory frameworks that are based upon a set of principles and there is some agreement on what these might include as shown in Box 1.1.

BOX 1.1   PRINCIPLES OF PUBLIC SERVICE

Principle	Definition
Selflessness	Public servants should make decisions and act solely in the public interest and not in their private interests including the interests of family, or friends or any other outside body or group. Public office should not be used for private gain.
Integrity	Public servants shall conduct their public, professional and private lives in a manner that will maintain and strengthen the public's trust and confidence in the ability of the public service to implement government policy. Public servants shall exhibit the highest standards of professional ethics and competence, working with skill, care and diligence and will carry out their duties with energy and goodwill, with efficiency and effectiveness.
Objectivity	Public servants should act impartially, make decisions based on merit and not give preferential treatment or discriminate on the basis of colour, race, nation, nationality, sex, language, religion, political opinion or other status or any other irrelevant consideration.
Accountability	Public servants are held responsible for their decisions and actions, ultimately by the governed. They must be prepared to give an account of their decisions and actions and submit themselves to whatever scrutiny is appropriate for their office.

Openness	Public servants exercise powers and distribute resources entrusted to them by the governed. They should be as open as possible about the decisions they make, taking care to justify their actions. Information should be restricted only when the wider public interest clearly demands it.
	Public servants may use and disclose information which is a matter of public knowledge or which the public has the right to access. However, in the course of their official duties, public servants will have access to information of a confidential or private nature, which is not authorized for disclosure.
Honesty	Public service is a public trust; the public entrusts the public service to act on its behalf and not pursue personal gain. The confidence and trust in, and respect for, the government by the governed depends upon public servants being honest and being seen to be honest. Public servants must keep the promises that they have made, be sincere and be free from deceit, extortion or corruption. Public servants may not use time, equipment and financial resources for personal use. They must not receive any gift or hospitality which may be construed as favouring an outside person or organization.
Leadership	Public servants should promote and support these principles by taking the lead and setting examples, demonstrating the highest standards expected of role models, both within the public service and within the community at large.
Respect for persons	Public servants should listen and respond to the needs of all those that they deal with in an official capacity in a timely manner, treating them with respect and courtesy.
Duty to uphold the law	Public servants should obey the law and should comply with any enactments, regulations or directives appropriate to the performance of their duties and as instructed to do so by the relevant authority. They should also respect any requirements of Human Rights legislation.
Exercising legitimate authority	Public servants are entrusted with power and authority. That power and authority should be exercised legitimately within the authority of office and with justice and equity. Public servants must not abuse their power and authority.

These regulatory frameworks generally consist of codes of conduct, audit functions, anti-corruption agencies, standards committees and ethics officers. We examine this framework in more detail in Chapter 6. At this stage it is important to note that the adoption of such frameworks appears to be universal with anti-corruption agencies in, for example, Hong Kong with its Independent Commission Against Corruption (ICAC), Sydney (similarly entitled ICAC), or New York City (Department of Investigation). Such agencies often balance investigation, retribution and education, and a key issue that we address below is to evaluate how successful they have been.

We should also mention the National Integrity System (NIS) approach of Transparency International (TI). Transparency International was founded in 1993 and is a global network of more than 90 locally established national chapters. These chapters combat corruption in their countries, bringing together relevant stakeholders from government, civil society, business and the media to promote transparency in elections, in public administration, in procurement and in business.

The organizational context

Our public services play host to a wide-ranging set of relationships, both formal and informal, that exist both inside the organization and between the organization and its external stakeholders. A key role for officials within these agencies is managing these relationships. In an idealized bureaucracy, such relationships are governed by hierarchy, formal rules and position within the organization. Despite the criticisms of bureaucracy, there is a role to be played by formal rules and relationships: accountability and responsibility are clearly located, discretion is kept to a minimum and entitlements are impartially administered. And yet, as we know, organizations are complex and dynamic and are made up of informal rules, norms and values. Here, relationships might be based upon trust, loyalty and obligations rather than formal contracts. The balances are between control and autonomy, between uniformity and discretion, between following the rules and the exercise of practical wisdom. We visit these balances in Chapters 6 and 7.

Public service organizations are subject, increasingly, to performance regimes. In education, policing, health, social services or the environment, public officials are subject to targets and their organizations are positioned in league tables depending upon performance. The authors of this book are not immune to such regimes. As university academics we are subject to performance reviews by our students, and our research output is judged according to the various rankings of the journals in which we publish. The allocation of our research time is based upon the quality of our outputs, the research income that we generate, the number of PhD students we supervise successfully and so on. There is no doubt that public officials should be held to account for the way in which public funds are spent; the problem is, as with all performance regimes, there are unintended consequences. Some consequences may be healthy, others may be unhealthy. There are numerous examples of statistics being manipulated to meet performance targets, of corners being cut, of 'gaming' and 'cream skimming', and we examine these in Chapter 8. There is a distinction to be made between assessing performance to help learning and development and assessing performance for control and to pass judgement. Too often, the latter drives out the former.

Further, the culture of the organization impacts individual behaviour. Lawton (1998) reports on the culture that prevailed in a police force of 'don't dob on your mates'. In other words, while these individual police officers might not have been corrupt, they condoned the petty corruption of a minority of their colleagues because loyalty to the team was more important. We examine culture, and organizational loyalty, in Chapter 5. Apart from culture, there are a host of legislations, protocols and policies that impact the individual public official in terms of equal opportunities, human rights, health and safety, anti-discrimination and so on. The extent to which such formal requirements are embedded in organizational cultures is, of course, a moot point.

The implementation of ethics frameworks is one that we examine in depth in Chapter 6 and 7. Our concern is not to present ethics as a series of 'do's' and 'don'ts'; rather, we are interested in how best to help public officials make better ethical decisions, both individually and collectively. We present the tools that are available, including ethics training, codes of conduct, social and ethical audit. We also draw upon understandings of the challenges involved in the implementation of any policy including resource, communication, leadership and competency issues. We also draw upon theories of ethics to help us in our decision-making.

ETHICAL THEORY

We have deliberately left a discussion of ethical theory to the end of our opening chapter. When we teach ethics to our local politicians or to our health-service professionals or our police officers, we do not start with a run-through of theorizing about ethics from, say, Aristotle through Kant through to Rawls. They would say, and rightly, 'Well, that is all very interesting but how does it help me when I am faced with a decision of how to allocate my scarce resources between equally needy patients?' or, 'I would really like to exercise my judgement in dealing with this offender but the law is absolutely clear on this point and I am going to arrest her.' We want to be able to help our public officials take individual responsibility and exercise their practical wisdom and recognize that an academic understanding of Aristotle's *Nicomachean Ethics* (1947), or Rawls' *A Theory of Justice* (1972) may not be entirely useful. Rather, our approach is to start with the kinds of decisions, and the context for those decisions, that officials make and to tease out underlying themes that might lend themselves to a consideration of different theoretical approaches to understanding ethics. We are not 'dumbing down' the importance

9

of ethical theory, but rather using theory to provide a background to making sense of the kinds of difficult decisions that our public officials make in their daily lives.

CONCLUSIONS

We have introduced some key concepts and presented a flavour of the issues that interest us and how we might explore them. The remaining chapters of the book provide a more in-depth discussion and address a number of key questions as identified in the chapter headings. We hope that you will find our discussions of interest and that you will reflect on your own ethical practices.

FURTHER READING

There are a number of books on public sector ethics that provide further reading.

Aristotle (1947) *Nicomachean Ethics*. Translated by W.D. Ross. New York: Random House.

Branigan, T. (2010) 'Rio Tinto Four Jailed for up to 14 Years by Chinese Court', *Guardian*, 29 March.

Cooper, T.L. (1998) *The Responsible Administrator: An Approach to Ethics for the Administrative Role*. 4th edition. San Francisco, CA: Jossey-Bass.

Doig, A. (1984) *Corruption and Misconduct in Contemporary British Politics*. Harmondsworth: Penguin.

Frederickson, G.H. and Ghere, R.K. (2005) *Ethics in Public Management*. Armonk, NY: M.E. Sharpe.

Garafolo, C. and Geuras, D. (2007) *Ethics in the Public Service: The Moral Mind at Work*. Washington, DC: Georgetown University Press.

Geuras, D. and Garafolo, C. (2011) *Practical Ethics in Public Administration*. 3rd edition. Vienna, VA: Management Concepts.

Huberts, L.W.J.C., Pijl, D. and Steen, A. (1999) 'Integriteit en Corruptive' [Integrity and Corruption] in Fijnaut, C.J.C.F., Muller, E. and Rosenthal, U. (eds) *Politie: Studies over haar Werking en Organisatie* [*Police: Studies on Its Operation and Organization*]. Alphen aan den Rijn, the Netherlands: Samsom, pp. 57–79.

Kelly, C. Sir (2009) 'MPs' Expenses and Allowances: Supporting Parliament, Safeguarding the Taxpayer'. Twelfth Report of the Committee on Standards in Public Life. London: HMSO. Cm 7724.

Lawton, A. (1998) *Ethical Management for the Public Services*. Buckingham and Philadelphia, PA: Open University Press.

Lewis, C.W. and Gilman, S.C. (2005) *The Ethics Challenge in Public Service: A Problem-Solving Guide*. 2nd edition. San Francisco, CA: Jossey-Bass.

Rawls, J. (1972) *A Theory of Justice*. Oxford: Clarendon Press.

Chapter 2

Ethical theory

What is the right thing to do and who is to say so?

LEARNING OBJECTIVES

By the end of this chapter you should:

- appreciate the usefulness of ethical theory by exploring the link between theory and practice
- understand different ethical theories and their impact upon the decisions of managers
- appreciate the distinctive ethics that professionals in the public service adopt
- be able to contrast ethics with values and show how the two are not necessarily the same.

KEY POINTS IN THIS CHAPTER

- Different ethical theories are available to us to guide, explain or justify ethical actions.
- For public officials, ethics becomes manifest in the decisions that they make; those decisions are bound by organizational constraints.
- Organizational ethics brings together individual, organizational and societal interpretations of ethics and these interpretations sometimes compete with each other.

KEY TERMS

- **Ethical decisions** – decisions made by public officials involving ethical judgement and having ethical consequences.
- **Consequentialist ethics** – focus on the consequences of an action such that an action is deemed ethical if there are more good consequences than bad.
- **Deontology** – the morality of an action is based on adherence to a rule and the right action to pursue is independent of the consequences of that action.
- **Rights** – cannot be overridden no matter what the consequences; entitled by morality, law, equity or duty.
- **Virtues** – dispositions to act, not just to think or feel in a certain way; for example, exhibit qualities of goodness, uprightness and morality.

INTRODUCTION

The theorizing of ethics clearly has a long history, from the Ancient Greeks through the Middle Ages to modern times. Its history has reflected different concerns, and with different relationships; between the individual and the city-State, between the individual and a Supreme Deity, between the individual and the community; and between the individual and the modern State. More recent relationships are between the individual and the organization. Two immediate questions arise: first, is there anything that we can learn from over 2,000 years of theorizing about ethics or are, for example, the issues raised by the Ancient Greeks too far removed to claim our attention? Second, are solutions generated to fit one context appropriate for another context? For example, can we use a model of personal relationships with family and friends, based on special obligations, to understand our relationship with the State that might be based upon more general obligations? We might wonder if there is a third kind of obligation that binds us to the organizations we work for, particularly as, for many of us, the organization may claim more from us in terms of time or commitments than family or friends.

We also raise the question of what kind of theory is ethical theory and what is the relationship between theory and practice? In the first instance, is ethical theory the kind of theory that can be tested empirically as true or false, or are our ethics a matter of personal taste? (Stewart 1991). In the second instance, how does theorizing about ethics inform our practice? Do we work it out as we go along or do we have a wardrobe full of ethical theories that we can call upon to wear depending upon the occasion? We discuss these issues below.

Much of traditional theorizing about ethics has predicated some view of human nature. Thus, one view argues that people are basically out for themselves and have to be constrained from pursuing their own self-interests at the expense of others. If not, in the graphic words of English philosopher Thomas Hobbes (1968), then life would be 'nasty, brutish and short'. Hobbes was writing in the context of the English Civil War. Nevertheless, we can legitimately ponder the extent to which there is a balance between the individual, society and the State, and also the organizations that they work for.

Finally, individuals might act in accordance with rules, or out of a sense of justice, or equality or freedom, or a sense of duty, or to satisfy individual conscience, or to benefit the most people. They might also act out of desire or need, because they are told to do so, out of fear, out of greed, selfishness or laziness. Equally they may act out of passion or love.

For our public officials, faced with making decisions on a daily basis, we are interested in the extent to which ethics informs those decisions. It is in the decisions that are made that we can judge the integrity of those officials. Sometimes, the decisions are routine, at other times they indicate a major switch in public policy; yet all decisions impact someone's life – that is the nature of the public services.

ETHICAL DECISIONS

How do individuals make decisions that have ethical implications and how do managers make decisions in their organizations that have ethical implications? Indeed what do we mean by ethical implications, what do they consist of, and implications for whom? Let us, first, discuss the concept of a decision as a way into answering these questions. Public officials make decisions all day and every day, and these decisions affect individuals as citizens, as taxpayers or as users of public services. Some decisions may be more important than others insofar as they impact more widely and more deeply; decisions on levels of taxation, on large-scale infrastructure projects or public health policies affect large sections of the population. In contrast a decision over whether to grant a planning application to an individual dwelling may affect only one family and their neighbours. Nevertheless that does not make the decision any less important for that small group of people. There are different types of decisions that public officials make – different in scale and impact. Should we use the same kinds of justifications for these different decisions? See Box 2.1 for suggested criteria such justifications may include.

BOX 2.1 JUSTIFICATIONS

- Are they based on an authoritative set of rules?
- Are they made by a legitimate authority?
- Do they demonstrate the efficient and effective use of taxpayers' money?
- Are decisions taken in the public interest and not the interests of an individual or small group?
- Are decisions taken according to the principle of fairness?
- Will more good than harm come out of the policy?
- Are decisions taken after appropriate consultations?

At the same time we may not accept justifications of a decision that demonstrate hypocrisy and double standards, dishonesty or lying; that are made on the basis of personal whim; that privileges private interests over public interests or that privileges pressure group interests; or does not fulfil promises or obligations. Similarly, we would expect the same general criteria to be applied when viewing policy decisions from an ethical point of view as from any other point of view (i.e. have all alternatives been considered; is the decision based on relevant and available evidence; have implementation issues been considered; are appropriate resources available, and so on).

Often the discretionary space that individual public officials have in making decisions is more limited than may be imagined. Decisions involving large-scale infrastructure projects, initiated by one government, are very difficult to change even by a new incoming government. Sunk costs invested in the project mean that it is extremely difficult to pull out of, say, building a new generation of attack vehicles for the armed forces, even though a new government may be less committed to military expenditure and despite the fact that a different perspective of the public interest may now prevail. We discuss the public interest in detail in Chapter 3.

We are interested in whether or not those working in public services take ethics into consideration when making decisions, what concept of ethics they hold, and whether the same concept is held by all types of individuals working in the public services. Recall that in the public services we can find members of the medical profession, the legal profession, engineers, architects, social workers, teachers, accountants and general managers. Is it likely that they will all share the same ethics as individuals? Does it really matter if they hold different ethical values as long as they share the same organizational ethos?

ETHICAL JUDGEMENT

The exercise of moral judgement has claimed the attention of scholars and has led to the development of measures to test it. Bringing together developments in the fields of psychology and philosophy, a number of studies have built upon original work by Kohlberg (1976) in refining and developing these measures. One useful definition is that of Rest, Thoma and Edwards (1997: 5):

> *Moral judgement* is a psychological construct that characterises the process by which people determine that one course of action in a particular situation is morally right and another course of action is morally wrong.

Kohlberg (1976) developed a schema for the moral development of individuals and this is shown in Box 2.2.

The implications of Kohlberg's work are that those lower down the stages are less ethical. In organizational terms does this mean that only those at the top of

BOX 2.2 KOHLBERG'S SCHEMA

Level I Preconventional

Stage 1 Based upon rules and authority and driven by the fear of punishment

Stage 2 Based upon the notion of fair and equal exchange and driven by individual instrumental purpose

Level II Conventional

Stage 3 Based upon mutual interpersonal expectations, relationships and the need to conform and driven by social expectations

Stage 4 Based upon conscience and to maintain the welfare of the group through carrying out one's duties

Level III Postconventional or principled

Stage 5 Based upon values and rights and recognizing the importance of the social contract

Stage 6 Based upon universal ethical principles and representing full moral maturity

N.B. Kohlberg considered Stage 6 reasoning to be rare.

organizations can reach stage 6? Now this may be stretching Kohlberg's thinking further than was intended, but the hierarchical framework has received much criticism (see Rest *et al.* 2000). The research has also been criticized for undervaluing the ethics of care (Gilligan 1982) and for offering little evidence that it is relevant for non-Western societies. We might also question the idea of moral development itself. Is there some ethical ideal that individuals strive for or do ethics result from the interplay of different values and negotiation between different groups in a particular society? A pragmatic approach to ethics might focus upon what is useful, rather than what is ideal (Rorty 1999).

Nonetheless, Kohlberg's schema has been refined, developed and revisited not just by Kohlberg himself but by subsequent researchers, and has led to other frameworks to assess moral judgement empirically (see, for example, Lovinsky, Treviño and Jacobs 2007; Rest *et al.* 1997; Rest 1979, 1986).

Two measures, the Defining Issues Test and the Managerial Moral Judgement Test, rely on hypothetical scenarios to elicit what respondents would do in a particular situation. The measures can be used for both the exercise of judgement by individuals in their managerial capacity and in their personal lives. The development of different measures suggests that individuals make different kinds of

---

BOX 2.3   COMPONENTS OF MORAL BEHAVIOUR

1.   Moral sensitivity – awareness of how our actions affect others.
2.   Moral reasoning or judgement – the ability to make critical decisions – application of general moral principles by individual moral agents to particular cases through a rational deductive process.
3.   Moral motivation – placing moral values above competing non-moral values.
4.   Moral character – having certain personality traits.

---

decisions, not just different decisions, depending upon the roles that we play. There are claims that managerial moral judgement involves lower levels of judgement compared to life outside of the organization. Yet there is an argument that the kinds of decisions we make reflect the kind of person that we are rather than the situation we find ourselves in. If this is the case then we can see how individuals may rebel when asked to do something by their organization that they disapprove of.

Rest (1994) identifies judgement as one of the four components of his schema of moral behaviour. See Box 2.3.

One concern for organizations is, can we foster judgement through ethical codes, through ethics training, through ethical culture? We return to ethical decision-making in Chapter 7 and build upon the introductory remarks expressed above.

ETHICAL THEORIZING

Within the constraints of this book we offer a general introduction to the key issues that have engaged researchers, and we point the way towards a more sophisticated discussion elsewhere. We cannot do justice to the subtleties of theorizing about ethics that have engaged scholars for so long, although a good place to continue is with Rachels and Rachels (2007) and, from the perspective of public administration, Garofalo and Geuras (2007). We recognize that at the same time, the definition of ethics and morality is contested. One minimum definition argues that

> Morality is, at the very least, the effort to guide one's conduct by reason – that is, to do what there are the best reasons for doing – while giving equal weight to the interests of each individual who will be affected by what one does.

(Rachels and Rachels 2007: 15)

In their examination of professional ethics, Banks and Gallagher (2009: 16) choose to use ethics and morality interchangeably and define ethics:

> Broadly speaking, we include within 'ethics' matters relating to the norms of right and wrong action, good and bad dispositions or 'character' traits and the nature of the good life.

We will endeavour to show the implications of different theories for our public officials.

Theorizing about ethics reflects developments in the philosophy of the social sciences more generally, with positivist and interpretive approaches evident. Does ethical theory involve the application and testing of hypotheses about human nature based upon some set of universal principles? Or do ethics reflect the context within which they are being practised, subject to competing interpretations and accommodated by different groups within a particular society? Thus, our basic questions will be concerned with whether we believe that the moral order required of us is derived from some sort of external source, perhaps laid down in an authoritative code or book, or whether it derives from human nature as a result of living with others in a society. Following on from this, are we motivated to act morally by something inside of us, such as a conscience, or are we compelled to act by an external force which might be fear of punishment, or desire for rewards? Not only that, but are there individuals or groups that have access to, as it were, moral wisdom, and to whom should we defer in our decisions?

Subjectivism

This is the view that it is for individuals to decide what is ethically right or wrong according to their chosen ethical principles, such that ethics are a purely personal matter. There is no guarantee that the chosen principles will be agreed to by anybody else. The advocates of subjectivism are wary of authoritarian pronouncements on ethics. Clearly the importance of moral autonomy cannot be over-stated, but should ethics be a matter of personal preference? If we claim that something is wrong, from this perspective, then are we merely expressing our feelings towards the act rather than judging the qualities of the act against some standard? There is no objective right and wrong, ethics is based upon sentiments and emotions and there is no way of choosing between disagreements. From this perspective ethics is used to express approval or disapproval, not right or wrong.

For some writers, part of the post-modern malaise is this focus on individualism, and for such writers how we relate to others is the key to understanding ethics (see Taylor 1991; Bauman 1993).

Given our discussion of public service motivation and the argument that public officials take on responsibilities for others and are committed to the welfare of others then subjectivism seems an unlikely basis for public service ethics.

Relativism

It is right for each society or social group to decide what is ethically right or wrong such that there are no universal ethical principles. There is no one best way so we cannot judge the ethics of another society or group for we have nothing to judge them by. Any attempt to impose our ethics on another society might be deemed ethical imperialism. Who are we to criticize the ethical practices of others? This line of argument is at the heart of discussions in business ethics concerning when does a gift, a traditional way of doing business in some countries, become a bribe? This is a problem in a world of international co-operation and agreements – how do we agree in basic values?

However, while accepting that there are different cultural outlooks, does that mean that there are no agreements in ethics? All societies seem to have, for example, some concept of justice, or obligations or equity or truth telling, or welfare even though they mean different things and take different forms in different locations. At least there is the possibility of a conversation, and we may overestimate the differences. Toleration of differences is important, but clearly it is a fine balance and we recognize that we should not be tolerant of everything. Many regimes do carry out grave injustices.

Consequentialist theories

These theories focus on the consequences of an action such that an action is deemed ethical if there are more good consequences than bad. There are various criteria for determining the balance. Utilitarianism is the best known of the consequentialist theories where an action is said to be morally justifiable if it leads to the greatest happiness of the greatest number. It is most closely associated with the work of the English philosophers Jeremy Bentham (1748–1832) and John Stuart Mill (1806–73). The first problem is to define happiness and to consider whether the same things make us happy. There has been a revival of interest in the concept of happiness as Box 2.4 indicates.

A version of utilitarianism is to be found in the techniques of cost–benefit analysis where it is argued that it is possible to weigh up all the consequences and benefits of a particular policy option through assigning a numerical weighting to all factors involved. In planning, for example, a new airport, a cost–benefit analysis will weigh up the costs and benefits of noise pollution, road congestion, threats to life and wildlife, threats to the environment, threats to the quality of life, the benefits of different forms of transportation and so on in as comprehensive a manner as possible. The concept of measurement is at the heart of the utilitarian approach. One immediate objection to this approach is how do you measure, for example, the quality of life? Utilitarianism is concerned with the maximization of good and the minimization of harm, howsoever defined. The good may be defined

BOX 2.4   MEASURING SUBJECTIVE WELL-BEING IN THE UK

The UK Office of National Statistics (ONS) carried out a survey to measure national well-being in the UK in 2011. The four questions and the results were:

1. When asked, 'Overall how satisfied are you with your life nowadays?' 76% of respondents were estimated to have a rating of 7 out of 10 where '0' is not at all and '10' is completely.
2. When asked, 'Overall, to what extent do you think the things you do in life are worthwhile?' 78% of respondents rated this at 7 or more out of 10.
3. When asked, 'Overall, how did you feel yesterday?' 73% responded with scores of 7 or more out of 10.
4. When asked, 'Overall, how anxious did you feel yesterday?' the ratings were more evenly spread, although 57% had ratings of less than 4 out of 10.

Given that the survey was undertaken at a time of recession, growing unemployment and debt it is surprising that not more people were experiencing anxiety.

Younger and older adults reported higher levels of satisfaction than those in their middle years and those with better health reported higher levels. Having a partner is also positively associated with 'life satisfaction', 'worthwhile', and 'happiness yesterday'.

All in all a fascinating study that will be extended in 2012.

Source: UK Office of National Statistics 2011

by utilitarians as pleasure or happiness. From this perspective the ends justify the means, and this is one of its problems because it seems to accept that individual rights can be ridden over as long as the benefits of so doing outweigh the costs. Thus, in a world of limited resources, it becomes possible to argue that rather than one patient receiving expensive, if life-saving care, that the resources are better spent treating many others with, perhaps, less expensive care even though they may not be suffering from life-threatening illnesses. Others argue that individual rights cannot be overridden no matter what the consequences.

Another problem is the difficulty in calculating all the consequences. Public policies have a nasty habit of throwing up unintended consequences and it is rare that we can predict the full impact of public policy. Not only that, but policies in the area of public health reform or education may take years to take effect and politicians, notoriously, work to a much shorter time frame.

Due to the problems associated with focusing on individual acts, a second version of utilitarianism focuses upon what general rules of conduct tend to promote general happiness, but this still suffers from the same problems of over-riding individual rights and the difficulty of assessing consequences.

We also need to ask, is it reasonable for individuals to consider all the consequences of their actions before they act? Our moral acts are often spontaneous with no thought of consequences; clearly when making public policies, more time is available for considered decisions, and collective decision-making may lend itself to a fuller understanding of the consequences and requires an understanding of public interest, which we address in Chapter 3.

Deontological theories

From this perspective the right action to pursue is independent of the consequences of that action. The right action would be to keep a promise, repay a debt, abide by a contract irrespective of the consequences. There are many non-consequentialist relationships such as friendship or parent–child relationships where special obligations arise in virtue of that relationship. Much of the thinking in this perspective is indebted to the work of German philosopher Immanuel Kant (1724–1804) who believed that an act is morally praiseworthy only if done neither for self-interested reasons nor as a result of natural disposition but rather from duty, much like our public official. Moral credit is given not just because someone performs the morally correct action but because it rests on duty. It is based on reason, not intuition, conscience or utility.

'I ought never to act in such a way except that I can also will that my maxim should be a universal law.' This is the famous categorical imperative. It is categorical because it admits of no exception and is absolutely binding. Reason is the same for all. It is imperative because it gives instructions on how to act; 'help others in distress', 'treat people fairly' or 'pay people equally'. Individuals and organizations cannot make an exception for themselves!

People can be treated as ends, for example, in order to achieve organizational goals but they should be treated with respect and dignity at all times so that they do not merely become servants or objects and are not used exclusively for the ends of others. It is about treating people as we would like to be treated ourselves – with respect and dignity. Some actions are wrong for reasons other than their consequences. For Kant, the features of an action that make it right are not dependent upon any particular outcome. There are many special relationships that depend upon commitment, trust and duty and these are non-consequentialist. Professional relationships are often seen in these terms. The doctor has a duty of care towards the patient, the teacher towards the student. Indeed the public service ethos involves a duty to act on behalf of the public. And yet a deontological approach, with an emphasis on procedures means that the wider concept of doing good is taken out of the equation altogether (Bauman 1993).

Of course such duties are, in practice, overridden. They can come into conflict with one another; we do break promises if we believe that to do so will do more good than harm, or to prevent suffering.

Virtues

Character-based theories have informed discussions of the ethics of public administration where the person rather than the action is the object of moral evaluation (see Cooper 1998). Distinct from focusing upon what kinds of action we perform is the question of what kind of person we are, a focus on 'being, not doing'. The reason why individuals perform good acts is because they are good people. For Aristotle (McKeon 1947: 1103a, 1–10), virtue is an excellence (*arête*) that can be divided into two types – intellectual and moral – reflecting the twin elements that make a person specifically human. Virtue is the means by which we become fully human because it allows us to fulfil our particular human end, generally taken to be the good life. This concept relates to Aristotle's belief that something can only be understood and fulfilled once it has reached its natural end, has fulfilled its purpose. The natural end for man is to achieve eudemonia. The good life can thus be recognized, understood and, most importantly, attained. Aristotle's virtue theory, therefore, necessarily prioritizes the good over the right, a distinction that remains crucial to virtue ethics today (Mangini 2000; Oakley and Cocking 2001). Moreover, Macaulay and Lawton (2006) hold that not only is virtue necessary for good governance, it is also political in a broader sense, as it cannot be cultivated or practised outside of the polis. A person can only achieve eudemonia inside the polis because it is only this particular form of association that facilitates the development of a person's human self. Thus, the individual achieves the good life within an association, and we return to this below when we examine the concept of organizational ethics.

Virtues are inclinations or dispositions to act, not just to think or feel in a certain way. They are not innate and must be cultivated and become habitual. A key question then is what are the virtues that might be relevant to public officials and do they change over time? Scholars have come up with a long list of virtues and these include benevolence, courage, rationality, fair-mindedness, prudence, respect for law, honesty, civility, self-discipline, trustworthiness and so on. Which ones of these might be relevant for our public official? Macaulay and Lawton (2006) identified a number of virtues of Monitoring Officers (ethics officers) in English local government to include ethical awareness, self-motivation, personal resilience, fearlessness, perseverance, political sensitivity, leadership skills and interpersonal skills.

Yet it is not always clear why some virtues should be more highly regarded than others as it depends upon the context and it becomes difficult to separate the person from the role. Thus, the qualities we look for in our teachers may be different from the qualities we look for in our police officers or our policy advisers. Not only that but our public officials may play different roles and different qualities might be required. Virtues may also take different forms. The courage of a policy adviser to stand up to a bullying politician is different to the courage that a front-line worker may face in the emergency services. And yet, it can be argued that some virtues are needed for any kind of human flourishing and these will include courage, sympathy, empathy, etc. (Gray 2009). At the same time,

> The moral courage required to hold a different view . . . remains everywhere in short supply.
>
> (Judt 2010: 160)

Justice and rights-based approaches

Recent debates on justice have focused upon the work of American scholar John Rawls and his masterpiece *A Theory of Justice* (1972). Rawls argues that a fair system of arrangements is one that the parties can agree to without knowing if it will benefit them personally. He posits a hypothetical original position where we make choices behind a 'veil of ignorance'. Individuals would choose two principles to govern moral action:

- Equality in the assignment of basic rights and duties.
- Social and economic inequalities are just only if they result in compensating benefits for everyone, particularly the least advantaged members of society.

Rawls argues that a rational person would not seek to maximize his or her gain based upon self-interest, but would choose a position that provided for the least advantaged. After all, the person making the choice might be a member of the least advantaged group.

Other approaches have focused upon rights and duties, particularly those of citizens, often expressed in terms of some kind of charter or constitution. A good example is the UN Declaration of Human Rights (1948) which argues in Article 22 that:

> Everyone, as a member of society, has the right to social security and is entitled to realization, through national effort and international cooperation, and in accordance with the organization and resources of each State, of the economic, social and cultural rights indispensable for his dignity and the free development of his personality.

It is a moot point how practical or enforceable such statements are and how universalistic the concept of rights proclaimed is.

In the rush to award rights and entitlements it is sometimes easy to forget duties. In universities students have the rights to representation on academic committees, rights of appeal and rights with respect to transparency of assessment procedures, and are entitled to receive feedback on their work. It is sometimes forgotten, not least by students themselves, that they may have duties to attend lectures, treat fellow students and tutors with respect, not to plagiarize and so on. Box 2.5 illustrates how one university department has drawn up its own charter of student rights and responsibilities.

And yet, according to Judt (2010: 88):

> However legitimate the claims of individuals and their rights, emphasizing these carries an unavoidable cost: the decline of a shared sense of purpose.

An ethics of care

One of the challenges to traditional ethics has come from the ethics of care that focuses upon relationships, rather than principles of duties. Dissatisfaction with Kohlberg's approach, as indicated above, led to the development of an ethics of care (Gilligan 1982). Interestingly, Gilligan's critique of Kohlberg is that it involves a gender bias, as women seemed to score significantly lower than men. The ethics of care is about moral development in terms of understanding our responsibilities and relationships. It consists of: flexible and trusting attitudes towards clients; a preference for oral communication; and no sanctions on clients (Stensöta 2010).

An ethics of care is interested in the quality of the relationships between, in our case, the public official and those that they engage with on a day-to-day basis. It is an interesting point that as the public services in many countries move closer to adopting business practices, does an ethics of care apply to the, *now*, customer, as it did to the, *then*, client or patient?

Notwithstanding that, the extent to which the feminist critique of ethics has conclusively shown that women are more likely than men to demonstrate an ethics of care is a moot point. Gender, race, education and age have all been studied as antecedents of an ethics of care but the research evidence is mixed (see Stensöta 2010).

ORGANIZATIONAL ETHICS

Can the organization, like the polis, be the place for human flourishing? Now our public officials work in organizations that consist of authority structures and hierarchies and where power is exercised. Within these organizations individuals have specific roles to perform and have duties that arise from their office. Thus, individual ethics are situated within an organizational context. Clearly individuals

BOX 2.5   STUDENT RIGHTS AND RESPONSIBILITIES

Students and staff at Everywhere University have a number of rights and responsibilities, including the right to be treated with respect and the right to be treated equitably.

Students' rights also include the right to equal learning opportunities, the right to access your teachers and the right to feedback on your work.

As an Everywhere Student you are expected to:

- be independent and self-motivated, accepting joint responsibility for your own learning
- be organized – know the dates and times of scheduled classes and attend accordingly
- be willing to work with others and to participate in discussions either in class or online
- take responsibility for all of your assessed work, ensuring it is submitted on time and ensuring it is free from plagiarism or cheating
- retain a copy of all assignment work submitted for assessment and hold it until a grade for the unit is published
- take the initiative and consult appropriately should any problems arise that may affect your academic performance
- respect the request from your lecturers and tutors regarding the use of mobile technology in class.

To ensure that there is a constructive learning environment for ALL students, lecturers and tutors may:

- exclude late arrivals to classes
- exclude students who are not prepared for their classes
- ask students to leave lectures or other classes if they are disrupting the learning experience of others.

Rude or aggressive behaviour is not acceptable from either students or staff.

do not enter organizations as moral blank sheets of paper, as it were, on which the organization then writes its own values and ethics. At the same time, the ethics and values of the organization make them, more or less, attractive to potential employees. We explore this in more detail when we look at public service ethos in Chapter 4 and public service culture in Chapter 5.

We might also wonder at the extent to which the good citizen or person is also the good manager and do we have different criteria for deciding upon 'goodness'. In the first instance those criteria might include loyalty to friends, generosity, kindness, even-temperedness and so on. In the second instance criteria might include reaching targets, being efficient, making effective use of limited resources or facilitating maximum performance from staff.

At the same time individuals will also belong to certain professions and these professions will have their own values and ethical considerations. It is easy to see how different loyalties will emerge, leading to possible conflicts. Similarly, different kinds of obligations will emerge for our public officials, from general obligations to obey the law and promote the public interest, to specific obligations to individual clients or citizens. So in looking at individuals within an organization or a profession we need to reflect upon the extent to which that organization or profession itself is ethical. To clarify: there might exist a code of honour amongst thieves that include loyalty, trust, honesty with each other, fair distribution of rewards and so on. All very laudable; but at the same time we might not think that thieving as a profession or a practice is very worthy. MacIntyre (1984) argues that justification of a practice is different to justification from within a practice. An organizational culture may encourage certain values and actions that are perfectly acceptable to those within the practice but when looked at from outside may not be acceptable to an external point of view. We touched upon a related issue earlier when we discussed ethical relativism (see also Box 2.6).

It is in organizations that a number of approaches discussed above are played out.

1. Organizational justice: organizations, particularly public service ones, rely upon procedural justice to ensure that individuals are treated equitably. Rules are formulated to guarantee equitable treatment such that public officials treat their clients impartially. Procedural justice involves fair processes, and distributive justice guarantees that rewards are fair. One issue that the public services seem to have avoided, to date, is outcry against executive pay that has bedevilled many private sector organizations.

   In practice, however, as Banks (2008) argues, there is often a focus on the individual practitioner making difficult decisions in cases that are constructed in ways that are decontextualized both from the character and the motives of the individuals involved, and the organizational, policy, political and social context. She argues that we are often presented with a picture of professional ethics as a rational process involving the application of ethical principles to practice, tackling difficult cases and making decisions. There may be inequalities built into the very structures of public organizations. Critiques of bureaucracy argue that bureaucratic ideals may be instrumental in approach, seeking the most rational and efficient ways of delivering on public service goals. In this sense public policy is about ends rather than means. And yet much of the public services is about engaging in relationships with a whole host of others whether they be students, clients, patients or whatever, and the quality of those relationships is crucial to the performance of those services. Ends and means are inextricably linked.

2. In terms of rights, organizations then are bound, in law, to pay heed to the rights of their employees in terms of health and safety regulations, employment law, anti-discrimination and so on. Given the full panoply of employment rights is there any guarantee that organizations will be 'good' employers?

3. In terms of principles, put simply, a deontological approach argues that we assess policy not on the basis of its consequences but whether or not it is consistent with certain agreed ethical principles. Ethical principles to guide policy analysis might include integrity, competence, responsibility, respect and concern for all stakeholders (see Box 2.7).

BOX 2.6 PRACTICES MAY HAVE THE FOLLOWING CHARACTERISTICS

1. Exhibit coherence and complexity
2. Socially established
3. Carried out through human co-operation
4. Involve technical skills which are exercised within evolving traditions of values and principles
5. Organised to achieve certain standards of excellence
6. Certain internal goods are produced in the pursuit of excellence
7. Engaging in human activity increases human power to achieve the standards of excellence and internal goods
8. Engaging in the activity systematically extends human conception of its internal goods

The internal goods are acquired by participating in the practice itself and may be unique to that practice. Thus, if beneficence is one of the internal goods of a practice of public administration then benevolence on the part of public officials will be required. The external goods are, for example, money, prestige or status and are the subject of competition with winners and losers.

'Organizations do tend to corrupt the practices which they support as a result of their focus on external goods.'

(MacIntyre 1984: 322)

BOX 2.7 PRINCIPLES THAT GUIDE MEDICAL AND HEALTH CARE

Autonomy – obligations to respect the decision-making capacities of individuals

Non-maleficence – avoid causing harm to others

Beneficence – obligation to provide benefits and balance benefits against risks

Justice – obligations of fairness in the distribution of benefits and risks

Source: Beauchamp and Childress (2008)

CONCLUSION

Our interest is in public officials working in, and for, public service organizations and making decisions that affect citizens individually or the public interest in general. Often they are guided by rules, because making decisions on a case-by-case basis would be too time-consuming and too complicated. Different functional areas require the exercise of different ethical considerations. Policy advisers at the top of government will need to exercise courage in 'seeking truth to power' to politicians who may not wish to hear views counter to their own. Front-line professionals will need to attend to individual rights and welfare and to be clear of the boundaries of their professional role (Banks 2008).

Our unit of analysis is not just the individual *qua* individual but the individual as part of a profession, performing certain duties within an organizational context. In this sense, ethical understanding needs a dimension of social explanation (Williams 1985). We also need to work out what is the nature of the activity that we are engaged in and is there an ultimate foundation to judge these activities against (i.e. the public interest)? As Vickers (1965: 33) states:

> To explain all human activity in terms of 'goal-seeking', though good enough for the behaviour of hungry rats in mazes, raises insoluble pseudo-conflicts between means and ends (which are thus made incommensurable) and leave the most important aspect of our activities, the ongoing maintenance of our ongoing activities and their ongoing satisfactions, hanging in the air as a psychological anomaly called 'action done for its own sake'.

Is public service its own reward, as an ongoing enjoyment of relationships with others both as colleagues, or as clients where making a difference to peoples' lives is important, or is there an ultimate purpose to it, in an Aristotelian sense?

27

REFERENCES

Aristotle (1947) *Nicomachean Ethics*. Translated by W.D. Ross. New York: Random House.

Banks, S. (2008) 'Critical Commentary: Social Work Ethics', *British Journal of Social Work* 38 (6): 1238–49.

Banks, S. and Gallagher, A. (2009) *Ethics in Professional Life: Virtues for Health and Social Care*. Basingstoke: Palgrave Macmillan.

Bauman, Z. (1993) *Postmodern Ethics*. Oxford: Blackwell Publishing.

Beauchamp, T. and Childress, J. (2008) *Principles of Biomedical Ethics*. 6th edition. Oxford and New York: Oxford University Press.

Cooper, T.L. (1998) *The Responsible Administrator: An Approach to Ethics for the Administrative Role*. 4th edition. San Francisco, CA: Jossey-Bass.

Garofalo, C. and Geuras, D. (2007) *Ethics in the Public Service: The Moral Mind at Work*. Washington, DC: Georgetown University Press.

Gilligan, C. (1982) *In a Different Voice: Psychological Theory and Women's Development*. Cambridge, MA: Harvard University Press.

Gray, J. (2009) *Gray's Anatomy: Selected Writings*. London: Penguin.

Hobbes, T. (1968) *Leviathon*. Edited by C.B. Macpherson. Harmondsworth, England: Penguin.

Judt, T. (2010) *Ill Fares the Land: A Treatise on Our Present Discontents*. London: Penguin.

Kohlberg, L. (1976) 'Moral Stages and Moralization: The Cognitive Development Approach' in Lickona, T. (ed.) *Moral Development and Behaviour: Theory, Research and Social Issues*. New York: Hott, Rhinehart and Winston, pp. 31–53.

Lovinsky, G.E., Treviño, L.K. and Jacobs, R.R. (2007) 'Assessing Managers' Ethical Decision-making: An Objective Measure of Managerial Moral Judgement', *Journal of Business Ethics* 73 (3): 263–85.

Macaulay, M. and Lawton, A. (2006) 'From Virtue to Competence: Changing the Principles of Public Service', *Public Administration Review* 66 (5): 702–10.

MacIntyre, A.C. (1984) *After Virtue*. Notre Dame, IN: University of Notre Dame Press.

Mangini, M. (2000) 'Character and Well-Being: Towards an Ethics of Character', *Philosophy and Social Criticism* 26 (2): 79–98.

McKeon, R. (ed.) (1947) *Introduction to Aristotle*. New York: Modern Library.

Oakley, J. and Cocking, D. (2001) *Virtue Ethics and Professional Roles*. Cambridge: Cambridge University Press.

Rachels, J. and Rachels, S. (2007) *The Elements of Moral Philosophy*. 5th edition. New York: McGraw-Hill.

Rawls, J. (1972) *A Theory of Justice*. Oxford: Clarendon Press.

Rest, J.R. (1979) *Development in Judging Moral Issues*. Minneapolis, MN: University of Minnesota Press.

—— (1986) *Moral Development: Advances in Research and Theory.* New York: Praeger.

—— (1994) *Moral Development in the Professions: Psychology and Applied Ethics.* Hillsdale, NJ: Lawrence Erlbaum.

Rest, J.R., Narvaez, D., Thoma, S.J. and Bebeau, M.J. (2000) 'A Neo-Kohlbergian Approach to Morality Research', *Journal of Moral Education* 29 (4): 381–95.

Rest, J.R., Thoma, S.J. and Edwards, L. (1997) 'Designing and Validating a Measure of Moral Development: Stage Preference and Stage Consistency Approaches', *Journal of Educational Psychology* 83 (4): 291–324.

Rorty, R. (1999) *Philosophy and Social Hope.* London: Penguin.

Stensöta, H.O. (2010) 'The Conditions of Care: Reframing the Debate about Public Sector Ethics', *Public Administration Review* 70 (March/April): 295–303.

Stewart, D.W. (1991) 'Theoretical Foundations of Ethics in Public Administration: Approaches to Understanding Moral Action', *Administration and Society* 23 (3): 357–73.

Taylor, M.C. (1991) *The Ethics of Authenticity.* Cambridge, MA: Harvard University Press.

Universal Declaration of Human Rights (1948) New York: United Nations.

Vickers, G. Sir (1965) *The Art of Judgement: A study of Policy Making,* London: Chapman and Hall.

Williams, B. (1985) *Ethics and the Limits of Philosophy.* London: Fontana Press/Collins.

Chapter 3

The public interest

Is there such a thing and what purpose does it serve?

LEARNING OBJECTIVES

By the end of this chapter you should have:

- understood the meaning and significance of the public interest
- considered key questions associated with the public interest
- analyzed its importance for public officials.

KEY POINTS IN THIS CHAPTER

- The public interest is a contested concept.
- There is a blurring of the distinction between public and private, particularly in the delivery of public services.
- The public interest is continually in tension with notions of citizenship, competing notions of the role of the State, and localized interests.

KEY TERMS

- **Public interest** – consists of the interests of a collectivity, usually the State, as distinct from individual private interest or group interests.
- **Networks and partnerships** – refer to the delivery of public services through partnerships with, or a network of, other organizations.
- **New public management** – a management philosophy adopted by governments that has brought about a wave of reforms since the 1980s. It is underpinned

by beliefs in, for example, greater competition in the public sector, private sector styles of management practice and measures of performance with greater emphasis on outputs.

■ **Trust** – citizens' expectations are based on trusting their elected representatives to act in the public interest. Trust is undermined when politicians are perceived to act in their own interests or those of a particular group.

INTRODUCTION

> Leaders of parties in cities have programs which appeared admirable. . . . but in professing to serve the public interest they were seeking to win prizes for themselves.
>
> (Thucydides 1954: 210)

Our fundamental understanding of politics, public policy, political philosophy and political ideology is based upon essentially contested concepts. Freedom, justice, autonomy and equality, to name but a few, are open to different interpretations. The possibility of testing these interpretations against some ideal or universal standard, to come up with some agreed definition is, itself, contested. Indeed it has been argued that everybody's values or positions are equally valid and there is no objective truth. The concept of the public interest shares these conditions, i.e. it is essentially contested and is difficult to universalize. However, we can elucidate its character by seeking to answer a number of key questions and these include:

–   What constitutes the public interest and how is it determined?
–   Under what conditions is it invoked?
–   How does it relate to other interests?
–   What guidance, if any, does it provide in making decisions?
–   Should it triumph over individual or group interests?
–   Has it come to be identified with particular interests?
–   Does it allow individual flourishing in its pursuit?
–   Does it rely upon a concept of citizenship?
–   Do public officials have a special duty to act in the public interest?

There are different ways in which we might seek to answer these questions and some of these are dealt with from different perspectives in other chapters. In this chapter, first, we can trace the historical usage of the term. Second, we can locate it within different traditions of political ideologies, such as liberalism or communitarianism. Third, we could clarify its relationship to other concepts such as democracy, citizenship, obligations and so on. Fourth, by analysing its leverage on individual motivation and reasons for acting, we can identify its role in decision-making.

We could also focus upon its legal use in defining a public interest defence and immunity from prosecution, and also its economic interpretation in terms of public goods arguments (see Hantke-Domas 2003). These legal and economic interpretations will take us too far away from our central questions and will not be pursued with any vigour. We will, however, return to our key questions throughout.

THE PUBLIC INTEREST OVER TIME

We come to discuss the concept of the public interest as part of a long tradition in political philosophy. That tradition, tracing back to the Greeks, is a rich source of debate concerning the role of the State, civil society and the relationships with individuals. Thus, the history of the public interest is the history of the relationship between the individual and the State, usually mediated by intermediary institutions, for example, family, community or clan. At the same time, the argument that there are distinct spheres of activity that separate individual or private interests from public interests has been contested. For the Greeks, the public realm, the polis, provides the sphere within which individual flourishing can take place. Nevertheless, there is a strongly held view in political philosophy that public policies are consequentialist in nature and these may conflict with the deontological underpinning of private morality (Hampshire 1978). Indeed, Machiavelli was quite clear that not only is it irresponsible but also morally wrong to apply to political action the moral standards that are appropriate to private life and to personal relations. From a different perspective the sociologist Richard Sennett (2002) traces the changing tensions between public and private spheres from the Enlightenment onwards and argues that the public realm is in decline when the private enters into it (see also Jordan 1989). The extent to which public and private can be clearly located is, increasingly, a moot point and we shall return to this below.

For other theorists, however, the State is coercive, and individual rights need to be protected from too much State interference. The question of what motivates individual men and women to live together in harmony has engaged political philosophy throughout time. One answer has been given by Finnis (1980: 305), who argues that

> an individual acts most appropriately for the common good, not by trying to estimate the needs of the common good 'at large', but by performing his [sic] contractual undertakings and fulfilling his other responsibilities to other individuals. . . . Fulfilling one's particular obligations . . . is necessary if one is to respect and favour the common good, not because 'otherwise everyone suffers', or because non-fulfillment would diminish 'overall net good' in some impossible utilitarian computation, or even because it would 'set a bad example' and thus weaken a useful practice, but simply because the common good is the

good of individuals living together and depending upon one another in ways that favour the well-being of each.

For the purposes of this chapter we will treat, as do others (e.g. Etzioni 2004), the public interest and the common good as synonymous; a much fuller treatment would explore the meanings given to each over time.

Notably, this (modern) quotation contains a number of enduring themes. First, the common good will emerge as a result of fulfilling particular obligations. Certainly the Kantian categorical imperative is concerned with treating people as ends in themselves, and this is how we reconcile our particular goals with universal moral requirements. Yet both Hobbes (1968) and Smith (1976), in particular, argued that nothing much good would come of pursuing the common good. In pursuing individual interests the common good will, eventually, result. For Smith, these interests were primarily economic in character, although with moral implications. Second, the quotation raises the issue of measuring the common good in some 'impossible utilitarian computation'. Third, and following on from the previous point, can the public interest be used as a guide to action, a reason for decisions? In a classical text, Flathman (1966: 4) argued that, at a minimum

. . . 'public interest' is used to express approval or commendation of policies adopted or proposed by government.

Clearly, and also as illustrated by the opening quotation to the chapter, there is a strong normative dimension to the public interest. Indeed, a normative approach to the public interest, setting an ethical standard, is identified by Denhardt and Denhardt (2007) as one of four possible approaches. They also identify an abolitionist stance, insofar as some theorist argued that since the public interest cannot be measured then it should not be used; at the same time a focus on individual choice is the best way of understanding public policy. A third approach, focusing on political processes, allows individual interests to be balanced. A fourth approach, shared values, sees the public interest arising out of shared interests and values.

Interestingly, at the same time, what constitutes the public realm is contested. It is not just about the State, but might include voluntary associations and intermediary institutions. We shall turn to communitarian arguments below. However, throughout the term's usage, the public interest has been seen as, either, an interest balancing approach, or as resulting from the promotion and protection of individual rights (Morgan 1994). The twists and turns of the relationship between State, civil society and the individual are well charted by Ehrenberg (1999). At this stage in our discussion we are left with a number of questions:

—   What is the appropriate role of the State?
—   What is the nature of citizenship?

- How can individual rights be balanced against duties to others?
- Who determines what might be in the public interest?
- How can individual interests be reconciled with group, community and State interests?
- How do we conceive of the public realm that is to serve the public interest?

Definitions and distinctions

The public interest can be seen in different ways: either as an abstract ideal or as realized in concrete decisions. As an ideal it is linked to the comprehensive purpose of an institution. In the liberal perspective, the public interest consists in upholding basic individual human rights such as the right of property, free speech, etc. In the utilitarian perspective it is taken to mean the welfare of a collective where welfare is regarded as the preferred satisfaction of the collective's individual members. The pluralist perspective sees the public interest as the winner between competing interests (see Bozeman 2007 for an excellent discussion of the different perspectives).

While the concept has a long history, it still features in much discussion of public policy as Exercise 3.1 illustrates.

EXERCISE 3.1   THE PUBLIC INTEREST AND BAE SYSTEMS: A MODERN TALE

BAE Systems is a major global defence contractor and is part of an industry, with some 60-plus sites in the UK that have been seen by successive governments as crucial to the UK economy. In the mid-1980s Saudi Arabia was keen to upgrade its defence systems and a series of deals were struck with the British government and BAE to supply, in particular, fighter aircraft. These deals were worth billions of pounds. As early as 1992, reports were emerging that millions of pounds were being paid to middlemen in kickbacks and bribes. Between 1997 and 1999, BAE set up offshore accounts in the British Virgin Islands and Switzerland to move large sums of money around.

In 2002 the OECD convention came into force, making it illegal to bribe foreign officials to win contracts.

In 2004 the UK Serious Fraud Office (SFO) began an investigation of BAE on charges of corruption. After a two-year investigation, on 14 December 2006 the Attorney General (the chief legal adviser to the government) decided that there were severe legal and technical difficulties in bringing any prosecution. It was also argued that the latest defence contract with the Saudis was in jeopardy with the loss of up to 100,000 jobs (no evidence was produced to support these claims) and the continuation of the investigation was not in the national interest.

At the time, the SFO was poised to gain access to Swiss banking files believed to contain information about BAE's offshore dealings with Saudi middlemen. The SFO argued that it could not be forced to drop an investigation on the grounds of commercial damage to British interests or even that it would sour relations with a foreign country. These excuses had been specifically ruled out by the OECD anti-bribery convention, to which the UK had signed up to. Prime Minister Tony Blair began a tour of the Middle East on 16 December 2006. Blair argued that good relationships with the Saudis are crucial in the fight against international terrorism. The director of the SFO decided not to proceed with the investigation and later stated that he had been under no pressure from the Attorney General not to proceed. The SFO continued investigating BAE's operations in other countries including the Czech Republic, South Africa and Tanzania. BAE later agreed to pay £30 million in a plea bargain deal over sales to Tanzania.

It was later announced, in the summer of 2007, that the US Department of Justice would carry out an investigation into BAE, resulting in a US$400 million plea bargain over jet fighter sales to the Czech Republic and Saudi Arabia.

Irrespective of the details of the case, can you identify a number of key issues that emerge for our discussion of the public interest?

Commentary

Areas to consider are as follows:

- Is the political interest of a prime minister or president the same as the public interest?
- What and whose interests are served primarily?
- Is the view of the public interest, argued for by the attorney general, certain MPs and the prime minister, shared by the British public at large?
- Does the geographical boundary of the public interest stretch to cover the global arena?

Let us start with a couple of definitions. Bozeman (2007: 12) argues that:

In a particular context, the public interest refers to the outcomes best-serving the long-run survival and well-being of a social collective construed as a 'public'.

Etzioni (2004: 2) suggests that:

> No society can flourish without some shared formulation of the common good. It provides criteria to draw on when the interests and values of the various groups that compose the society pull them in conflicting directions.

So, there needs to be some shared formulation, a set of criteria and a recognition that interests will pull in different directions. What are the criteria that determine the common good and what might these different interests be? The answer to the first question is not immediately obvious. To say that it constitutes the sum of individual or group interests within a given territory does not help very much. Clearly there are common interests and there are public goods in the shape of common land, environment, defence, etc. Moreover, is it – as it was for the Greeks – constitutive of the good life where human flourishing could take place? In one sense, it has been argued, it is. For some theorists, the public interest is not an end state but a process and in constituting a process it allows citizens to engage with each other. Thus it is inextricably linked with citizenship, and provides meaning to democratic deliberations. It constitutes a process through which collective values are worked through rather than defining these in advance (Honohan 2002). Thus, the public interest balances different values and interests (Lewis 2006). It does not identify with particular interests. It is not the same as local or community interests. Public interest results from a dialogue within which different voices or interests can be heard, and public officials have a duty to help citizens articulate their voice (Denhardt and Denhardt 2007). As we know, however, this dialogue is flawed insofar as some interests have louder voices than others and some are excluded altogether. The public interest, then, can never be static but will respond to different interests.

What might these other interests be? As individuals we often act in the interests of others, including family, friends and colleagues; there is clearly a difference between acting in the public interest and acting in the interests of known others. However, we also act in the interests of strangers, of people that we do not know and, for example, share the same planet, future, public space, values and/or goals. Honohan (2002: 268) argues that we should not have to choose between analogies of either friends or strangers, but, rather, use the analogy of a colleague:

> Colleagues find themselves as relative equals in an institution or practice. Yet they are diverse and relatively distant from one another, and may have no close knowledge of, or strong feelings for, one another. They do not generally choose one another, but yet have common concerns rooted in a common predicament.

Such relationships can give rise to special obligations out of consideration, concern and trust. The idea of particular obligations, rather than universal or general obligations, is at the heart of communitarian thinking as expressed by Etzioni (2004). Common good equals the shared interests of citizens; it contrasts with the interest that a person has in occupying a certain role. As citizens we will need to exercise restraint, show solidarity with other citizens, be aware of how we relate to others and recognize the existence of interdependencies (Honohan 2002). Our interests as citizens are different in kind from our interests as parents or as motorists or whatever role we choose to perform (see Pettit 2004). How should people's common interests as citizens be defined? The communitarian view distinguishes the obligations of members of communities from those of citizens of the State. Not only that but particular obligations take precedence over universal obligations. According to Etzioni (2004: 11):

> On all matters not governed by universal rights, however, particularistic obligations hold sway.

There is a danger that Etzioni recognizes, however, that such obligations might turn into cronyism, nepotism and favouritism.

The State clearly does protect the interest of certain groups within society – notably, in our example, the defence industry. Do economic interests trump other kinds of interests? Some interests have come to be identified with the interests of the State – economic and security – and these two key interests have come to define, in many ways, the modern State. If individual rights suffer then, it is argued, so be it. The State defines the public interest because individuals and communities act in their own interest. It is only the state that can do this.

Why should groups put their own interests aside? Possibly because on other decisions they will get their own way, but this presupposes that all decisions are of equal importance to the stakeholders. Or perhaps they will gain some advantage greater than if they were to continue to pursue their own interests. The role of the State may be seen as honest broker, protecting the public interest, and in so doing individual interests, from group interests. This role would depend upon all stakeholders recognizing the State as the legitimate and authoritative decision-maker or broker.

Honohan (2002) argues that individuals carry out their activities within a range of practices in which they interact with each other and which give, or fail to give, recognition to certain goods (but there must be agreement in what goods are important!). The good of one is dependent upon the good of others. The good of citizenship lies in active participation in collective self-determination, not in the pursuit of some greater good. Also, it is the opportunity, not the actuality that is important. Yet, not everybody chooses to avail themselves of the opportunity. Such arguments are based upon a traditional notion of citizenship, a notion that is itself contested. We might also need to rethink our notion of citizenship. Citizenship may be becoming uncoupled from the State. Bang (2005) identifies expert citizens who are the 'new professionals' in voluntary and other agencies and 'everyday makers' who are engaged in 'roll-on, roll-off' activity and who might think globally but act locally on specific projects. Theirs is not a full-time engagement with the

State or its agencies but varies depending upon localized interests. In terms of the relationship between the different roles that we play as citizens, customers, as members of a family, a sect or a tribe, then we might like to think that citizenship rights would trump, say, customer sovereignty. The Greek concept of citizenship was instituted and acted out in the bounded spaces of the city-State. Yet for the Greeks, public life was not something distinct from other spheres but the highest of aims (see Painter and Philo 1995). Citizenship then, has to offer more than could be gained through market power as a customer. Yet we are still left with the question of how to engage individuals in civic life. Perhaps we need to rethink our notion of citizenship: Marston and Mitchell (2004) explore citizenship as non-static, non-linear, social, political, economic and legal; it is not a finished product but something which expands and contracts. Citizenship formations are a product of the interaction of civil society and the State and can be interpreted in multiple ways. It is not just about voting in an election every four to five years.

We may also wonder at the extent to which individuals act according to the public interest. Public interest provides no guidance when faced with a difficult decision. We act with respect to other persons, not to some abstract notion of a public interest. In this sense, public interest takes away from treating individuals as ends in themselves. Clearly private interests can be dressed up as public interests, as our opening quotation from Thucydides illustrates.

The challenge is to convince us that acting on behalf of individual or group interests is in all our interests. This is the trademark of politicians throughout the ages from Thucydides to Blair (to paraphrase our opening quote, 'When politicians start talking about the public interest, run for the hills'!). The public interest is presented as a value and is clearly an argument that is used in persuasion and should be judged, perhaps, by its ability to persuade us as part of a tradition of understanding politics. What convinces us? Not a utilitarian demonstration of costs and benefits but the force of the argument and the sincerity of the speaker and our trust in them! Under what conditions is the public interest invoked? When there is likely to be suspicion over motives? When it is felt that a decision might be seen as favouring the interests of individuals or groups?

Reasons may be valid and seen as appropriate, but may be given different weighting. In our example do we not only accept Blair's reasoning but also give it the same weighting? We might just think that it is wrong, irrespective of consequences, to bribe officials to win contracts.

The changing landscape of public service delivery

The concept of the public interest is multi-faceted, embracing a notion of citizenship, a concern with a common good, a distinction between public and private interests and a theory of human nature. The concept is used to describe, justify and gain support for decisions that are taken by public officials. Decisions taken 'in the public interest' are said to be better decisions, in some sense, than those taken in support of private or group interests. The public interest is at the heart of our understanding of democracy and provides the rationale for much public service delivery. It is linked to conceptions of justice, fairness and equity and requires compassion, empathy, altruism and benevolence.

As such we want to view developments in the delivery of public services through the prism of the public interest. There has been enough written on the impact on a public service ethos of the changing landscape of public service delivery (Lawton 1998; Pratchett and Wingfield 1996). In this section we, in brief, examine what motivates public officials and what is their sense of obligation. At the same time we need to consider why we should trust them to act on our behalf. There is also a growing demand for the co-production of public services where individuals other than elected or appointed officials, or managers of non-public organizations, are involved in the delivery of public services. There is a growing army of volunteers (sometimes paid in the form of expenses and allowances) that are involved in the governance of schools and hospitals, the care of the elderly or the committees of the local authority. What motivates them?

There is a fundamental contradiction at the heart of the duties of public officials: the balance between commitment to individuals and to groups. There is also a distinction to be made between the overall public interest, which is the duty of the State to support and protect, and a public interest as perceived by multitudes of public officials (O'Toole 2000). It is, for example, too simplistic to argue that managers look after the interests of all and professionals look after the interests of their patients or clients without consideration of the greater good. Officials have a general duty of beneficence to do what one can to help others (Moore 1981). Yet this may be in conflict with the more general requirement to consider the consequences of policies they advocate or implement. They must balance the duty of beneficence to individuals with their duty to serve the public interest. We might expect our public officials to act out of a duty of care towards patients and clients, not customers or consumers. To act out of altruism and beneficence, or even, as public choice theorists would have us believe, rational self-interest.

Of course, the distinction between citizens, customers and users has become more critical in recent years, with the language of the customer dominating our public discourse, making the concept of the public interest even more problematic (see Office of Public Services Reform 2002).

Motivation

How do appointed public officials, themselves, perceive their role? What motivates them? Public officials perform a range of different functions and roles and will have different perceptions on what the duties of a public official are. Within the local government context we find a range of different types of professional imbued with their own ethos (see Pratchett and Wingfield 1996), middle managers and front-line staff working in a range of core and non-core service areas, carrying out both statutory and non-statutory duties.

However, Le Grand (2003) distinguishes between public officials as Knaves, who act in their own self-interest, and Knights, who help others for no private reward and, indeed, sometimes to their own disadvantage. Knightly activities do not necessarily lead to the public good; the doctor who looks after patients may not have the same agenda as the policy-maker. Thus, particular obligations come into conflict with more universal ones. Also the status of the Knight can change if the Knavely behaviour seems to be rewarded.

More generally, it has also been argued that individuals do have different capacities for ethical reasoning (Kohlberg 1976), and officials who have reached the principles or postconventional levels of ethical reasoning will act in the public interest, as discussed in Chapter 2.

There is evidence to suggest that politicians, more generally, seek public office for different reasons and have different ethical motivations. Mancuso (1995), for example, constructs a taxonomy of basic ethical types amongst Members of Parliament, namely puritans, servants, muddlers and entrepreneurs.

All of these issues raise questions concerning the role and definition of the public interest as defined by those working within and for the public services. Recent evidence seems to indicate that the search for agreement in a set of common values is problematic. The Audit Commission (2002: para 35:17) finds that public and private sector managers working in partnership are motivated by different goals and that the most important factor in joining the public service is '*to make a difference*':

> But for a few making a difference is not the same as 'working for the common good', which can only happen in not-for-profit sectors. For this group, working for society as a whole, rather than those who can afford to pay for treatment or services, or for the benefit of shareholders, is a crucial motivation. And for some respondents, although serving the public had not been their main reason for joining the public sector, it was something they came to appreciate and value.

The opportunity to make a difference to service users and local communities is the biggest single reason why people join the public sector. How this plays out in terms of individual outcomes is not always obvious. However, according to the Audit Commission, individuals are attracted to the job rather than the sector, once again implying a particular, rather than general obligation.

At the same time, public officials are working more and more with their colleagues in other parts of the public service and with private sector managers and organizations, whose interests may be towards the success of their own organizations rather than in an abstract public interest.

A related development however, is the role increasingly played by independent lay members on a range of public bodies and committees. For example, local standards committees with the responsibility of upholding ethical standards in UK local authorities must include independent members; what incentives do individuals have to step forward and volunteer for such roles given the increasing demands that are placed upon them by new regulatory requirements? While a range of public services in health, education and social services are 'co-produced' with lay volunteers there is evidence that the increasing demands placed upon them is making recruitment difficult. Moreover, how does this growing army of volunteers define serving the public interest? Is the public interest the same as local interest? Is the school governor acting in the public interest and is this the same as community interests? We do not know enough about this group of people. Therefore, Chapter 4 is devoted to the important issue of public service motivation, to follow on from this discussion.

Networks and partnerships

At the organizational level, public service organizations engage in a range of different types of relationships with a host of other organizations, public, voluntary and private. Such relationships need to be built around a common set of values and common goals.

As public services are delivered in a variety of different ways through different types of organizations, locating the public interest becomes more problematic, and it is rarely the case that there is agreement in common values. Thus, the delivery of public services through networks poses new challenges for public officials. Management activities are directed towards improving and sustaining interaction between the different actors involved and uniting the goals and approaches of the various actors. Kickert, Klijn and Koppenjan (1997: 44) define network management as

> promoting the mutual adjustment of the behaviour of actors with diverse objectives and ambitions with regard to tackling problems within a given framework of inter-organizational relationships.

The key phrase is 'diverse objectives and ambitions'. Thus managers have to:

— Manage across jurisdictions: organizations have legitimate interests and expect to have their autonomy respected. Different definitions of the proper remit of public services activities are held by different agencies. Management under such circumstances requires the ability to balance both the goals of the individual organization and those of the network as a whole. The manager needs to recognize that members of a network in the public services may represent separate and distinct and legal entities with different systems of accountability.
— Manage different stakeholders: common interests need to be identified and perceived as being more important than conflicting interests. Managing

> stakeholder interests means enforcing commitments across organizational and territorial boundaries.

- Manage implementation: a common base of information, standards, monitoring, and to overcome difference in organizational design and structure.
- Manage the exchanges: this means respecting confidences and building trust as well as putting in place appropriate formal agreements (see Rose and Lawton 1999).

Involvement of the private sector in public service delivery raises its own issues with respect to the public interest, not least because accountability mechanisms might be weakened. As Hebson, Grimshaw and Marchington (2003: 490) argue:

> Overall, accountability takes on a very different form in PPPs [public private partnerships] compared to that associated with traditional public administration. As the partnership develops and the public sector managers become more adept, accountability is increasingly framed in terms of meeting contract specifications; all decisions are contested, since the traditional basis for rule-making has been undermined, and opportunistic behaviour enters into the mainstream.

At the same time we might ask, should private sector organizations be held to account in the same way and should they be forced to disclose what might be commercial-in-confidence information?

Achieving the balance between individual, group and network interests is clearly difficult. Where this balance should lie has become increasingly confused, as regulatory regimes and the modernization agenda have consequences, both intended and unintended, for individual commitment. Not only that, but it is a moot point that this balancing act is what public officials do, or indeed should do. Individuals make decisions within the context of a set of rules and processes and it is these that inform their actions.

Not only do networking and partnerships pose challenges for officials, but also for politicians. Local politicians are likely to serve on a number of different boards, either as individuals or as representatives of their local authority. The possibility of conflicts of interests are increased and the Standards for England, the body charged with overseeing the conduct of local politicians, has examined a number of cases of conflicting responsibilities among local councillors.

Thus, new public governance and management not only represent structural shifts in the way things are done, but are about new ways of addressing, interpreting and disseminating what 'the public' is, what is in its interest and how it should be 'served'. What this might mean is a real political issue, especially given that what constitutes the boundaries between the State, the market and civil society is being challenged.

Many argue (see Shaw and Williams 2004) that the new entrepreneurialism and public management brings benefits in increasing the capacity of public agencies to tackle complex development problems because traditional government boundaries, interests and response capabilities are not sufficiently attuned to, and do not neatly map on to, the multiplicity of underlying social processes. Shaw and Williams (2004) also echo the concerns of others by arguing that these types of initiatives result in a troublesome blurring of the boundaries between the public and the private. The problem is that rather than transcending inequalities in society, partnerships could reinforce them by representing the interests of the most powerful partner more effectively. The payback for commercial private interests in this scenario would be greater access to public service delivery and the legitimation of their own priorities as being synonymous with the public good.

Trust

We expect our public figures to be virtuous in some form or another, unless of course we are completely cynical (and there is plenty of evidence to justify such a position). We have role models and they take on iconic status. We have high expectations of them and feel let down when these expectations are not met. One concern is with the extent to which we trust individuals in the form of elected and appointed public officials, and professionals to act in the public interest and the extent to which we trust organizations to act in the public interest. It is particularly appropriate that networks and partnership of public, private and voluntary organizations address this issue.

Public opinion surveys typically locate public service professionals, particularly the medical profession, as the most trusted, with politicians much lower; this, regardless of the well-publicized misdemeanours of individual members of the professions. Notwithstanding the views of the general public, the regulation of conduct of those working in, and for, the public services has been tightened by central government legislation, and is likely to continue (see O'Neill 2002).

Despite lack of trust in politicians and public officials, the institutions of democracy continue to be supported. Courts of Law, administrative appeals, the Ombudsman, etc. can provide a counterpoint to arbitrary decision-making by officials. Systemic failure resulting in 'tyranny of the majority' or the exclusion of relevant interests would cause more problems than lack of trust in individual politicians.

Still, trust relationships are built upon expectations; part of the reason why we mistrust politicians is that they do not keep promises. At the same time, and linked to this is performance: if public officials perform their duties as they are supposed to then we will trust them when they make promises to us (see Lawton 2002). If, as suggested above, that measuring the public interest is problematic then perhaps the 'abolitionists' (in Denhardt and Denhardt's terminology) are right to have nothing to do with it.

Public and private

> When a man assumes a public trust, he should consider himself as public property.
>
> attributed to Thomas Jefferson (1807)

In many countries, it is taken as a given that those seeking public office have public duties and in such countries we are quick to chastise those who seek public office for private gain. In other countries election to office is perceived as a vehicle for furthering business interests, holding no conception of a possible conflict of interest between public duty and private interests.

At the same time, as we have argued, the distinction between public and private interests has become blurred as the regulation of individual conduct and the promotion of ethical standards have become more pronounced. Such concerns are unlikely to go away. Moreover, the private lives and interests of public officials continue to engage our attention. In research carried out for the Committee on Standards in Public Life, the National Centre for Social Research (2002: 19) found that:

> There was a recurrent view that where an individual's private life may have a bearing on their public role then it was in the public interest to know about it. However, given that the aspects of private life deemed relevant would differ considerably between each public office holder, there was broad acknowledgement that in practice such a requirement would be difficult to implement.

Later research for the same Committee found that the public places a high priority on officials acting solely in the public interest, although politicians setting a good example in their private lives was not considered important (BRMB Social Research 2004).

Just as the boundaries between the public and private sector have become blurred, so is the distinction between public and private lives. A consultation carried out by the former Office of the Deputy Prime Minister (2004) on a model code of conduct for local government employees raised the issue of the boundary between private life and public interest, and a key question was, 'Which public officials should register their interests?' Should it be all those above a certain grade, or all those who are involved in procurement, licensing and land planning?

CONCLUSIONS

At a time when public sector performance is high on the agenda of all States, links between commitment, motivation and performance need to be more firmly established in research on public sector organizations. In the case of public service organizations, commitment on the part of public officials to their customers or clients, in particular, and citizens generally, is crucial. At the same time high performance in responding to their various needs of the various stakeholders is required. Yet commitment to a public service ethos and high performance, however defined, may be in tension. As public service managers are enjoined to be more entrepreneurial and innovative in their activities, there are fears that traditional notions of accountability and probity may be undermined.

If the public interest is best served by public officials balancing the interests of key stakeholders through network governance then it needs to be recognized that customers, consumers, citizens and clients enjoy different relationships with the State, and perhaps the most important one is not the role of citizen. We may ask to what extent the obligations of public officials are always of the same kind. Not only that, but public officials make decisions, and fulfil obligations and duties, within a framework of professional and organizational practices. These practices are somewhat removed from an abstract notion of the public interest. Few of them reach the heady heights of a Kohlbergian principled State. Further, if public interest is seen as emerging from a process then officials have a duty to create the space for deliberative engagement. For many this will be problematic as it will involve giving up power and professional status. At the same time, under conditions of moral and cultural diversity there is no single interpretation of the common good that is authoritative.

Notwithstanding the difficulties, the public interest will continue to claim our attention and will continue to be part of our language; it will be used with caution unless politicians can increase the trust that we have in them. However, it recognizes that we have to live together and that we are connected globally. People face a common predicament and have common concerns, both now and in the future and we are thrown together historically with a wide range of interdependencies. It relies upon a new meaning of citizenship that recognizes cultural diversity and shifting territorial boundaries. This is where its importance lies.

At the same time it is unlikely that it will allow individual flourishing; we find meaning in many other activities and political activity is unlikely to be, for most people, the ultimate form of human self-realization. Being a citizen does not have to mean abandoning other identities or values. Yet Urry (2000), for instance, notes how the new mobility that is sweeping the globe is dissolving the private interests of consumers and the public rights and obligations of citizens. He focuses on how global developments like the rise in consumer rights, the increased delivery of public services by private organizations and the way in which the State has formed governance partnerships with private, voluntary and quasi-public organizations have impacted on public life. Under these new arrangements, Urry argues that in reality a Marshallian (1992) depiction of citizenship is being replaced by a more hybrid 'consumer citizenship' and that the role of the State has changed from one of directly delivering public services to one of regulating the performances and standards of the various organizations that now do. This is an evolving set of circumstances, and the hybridity to which Urry (2000) refers is not a completed state of affairs by any means, but is constitutive of an ongoing struggle between varied private and public rights and interests.

REFERENCES

Audit Commission (2002) *Recruitment and Retention: A Public Service Workforce for the Twenty-first Century.* London: Audit Commission.

Bang, H. (2005) 'Among Everyday Makers and Expert Citizens' in Newman, J. (ed.) *Remaking Governance: Peoples, Politics and the Public Sphere.* Bristol: The Policy Press, pp. 159–78.

Bozeman, B. (2007) *Public Values and Public Interest: Counterbalancing Economic Individualism.* Washington, DC: Georgetown University Press.

BMRB Social Research (2004) 'Survey of Public Attitudes Towards Conduct in Public Life', prepared for the Committee on Standards in Public Life. London: BMRB Social Research.

Denhardt, J.V. and Denhardt, R.B. (2007) *The New Public Service: Serving not Steering.* New York: M.E. Sharpe.

Ehrenberg, J. (1999) *Civil Society: The Critical History of an Idea.* New York: New York University Press.

Etzioni, A. (2004) *The Common Good.* Cambridge, MA: Polity Press.

Finnis, J. (1980) *Natural Law and Natural Rights.* Oxford: Clarendon Press.

Flathman, R.E. (1966) *The Public Interest: An Essay Concerning the Normative Discourse of Politics.* New York: John Wiley and Sons.

Hampshire, S. (1978) 'Public and Private Morality' in Hampshire, S. (ed.) *Public and Private Morality.* Cambridge: Cambridge University Press, pp. 23–54.

Hantke-Domas, M. (2003) 'The Public Interest Theory of Regulation: Non-Existence or Misinterpretation', *European Journal of Law and Economics* 15 (2): 165–94.

Hebson, G., Grimshaw, D. and Marchington, M. (2003) 'PPPs and the Changing Public Sector Ethos: Case-study Evidence from the Health and Local Authority Sectors', *Work, Employment and Society* 17 (3): 481–501.

Hobbes, T. (1968) *Leviathan.* Edited by C.B. Macpherson. Harmondsworth, England: Penguin.

Honohan, I. (2002) *Civic Republicanism.* London: Routledge.

Jackson, P.M. (2001) 'Public Sector Value: Can Bureaucracy Deliver?', *Public Administration* 79 (1): 5–28.

Jordan, B. (1989) *The Common Good: Citizenship, Morality and Self-Interest.* Oxford: Blackwell.

Kickert, W.J.M., Klijn, J.-E. and Koppenjan, J.F.M. (eds) (1997) *Managing Complex Networks: Strategies for the Public Sector.* London: Sage.

Kohlberg, L. (1976) 'Moral Stages and Moralization: The Cognitive Development Aproach' in Lickona, T. (ed.) *Moral Development and Behaviour: Theory, Research and Social Issues.* New York: Holt, Rinehart and Winston.

Lawton, A. (1998) *Ethical Management for the Public Services.* Buckingham: Open University Press.

—— (2002) 'Trusting In, and Trust Within, the Public Services', *Teaching Public Administration* XXII (2): 1–13.

Le Grand, J. (2003) *Motivation, Agency and Public Policy: Of Knights and Knaves, Pawns and Queens.* Oxford: Oxford University Press.

Lewis, C. (2006) 'In Pursuit of the Public Interest', *Public Administration Review* 66 (5): 694–701.

Mancuso, M. (1995) *The Ethical World of British MPs.* Montreal: McGill-Queen's University Press.

Marshall, T.H. (1992) 'Citizenship and Social Class' in Marshall, T.H. and Bottomore, T. *Citizenship and Social Class.* London: Pluto Press, pp. 55–93.

Marston, S.A. and Mitchell, K. (2004) 'Citizens and the State: Citizenship Formations in Space and Time' in Barnett, C. and Low, M. (eds) *Spaces of Democracy.* London: Sage, pp. 93–112.

Moore, M.H. (1981) 'Realms of Obligation and Virtue' in Fleishman, J.L., Liebman, L. and Moore, M.H. (eds) *Public Duties: The Moral Obligations of Government Officials.* Cambridge, MA: Harvard University Press, pp. 3–31.

Morgan, D.F. (1994) 'The Public Interest' in Cooper, T. (ed.) *Handbook of Administrative Ethics.* New York: Marcel Dekker, pp. 151–178.

National Centre for Social Research (2002) *Guiding Principles: Public Attitudes Towards Conduct in Public life.* London: National Centre for Social Research.

Office of the Deputy Prime Minister (2004) *A Model Code of Conduct for Local Government Employees: A Consultation Paper.* London: ODPM.

Office of Public Services Reform (2002) *Reforming our Public Services: Principles into Practice.* London: Office of Public Services Reform.

O'Neill, O. (2002) 'A Question of Trust' BBC Radio 4, The Reith Lectures.

O'Toole, B.J. (2000) 'The Public Interest: A Political and Administrative Convenience?' in Chapman, R.A. (ed.) *Ethics in Public Service for the New Millennium.* Aldershot: Ashgate Publishing, pp. 147–54.

Painter, J. and Philo, C. (1995) 'Spaces of Citizenship: An Introduction', *Political Geography* 14: (2) 107–20.

Pettit, P. (2004) 'The Common Good' in Dowding, K., Goodin, R.E. and Pateman, C. (eds) *Justice and Democracy.* Cambridge: Cambridge University Press, pp. 150–69.

Pratchett, L. and Wingfield, M. (1996) 'Petty Bureaucracy and Woolly-minded Liberalism? The Changing Ethos of Local Government Officers', *Public Administration* 74 (4): 639–56.

Rose, A. and Lawton, A. (eds) (1999) *Public Services Management.* Harlow: Pearson Education.

Sennett, R. (2002) *The Fall of Public Man.* London: Penguin (first published in 1977).

Shaw, G. and Williams, A.M. (2004) *Tourism and Tourism Spaces.* London: Sage Publications.

Smith, A. (1976) *An Inquiry into the Nature and Causes of the Wealth of Nations Vol. 1.* Edited by Cambell, R.H., Skinner, A.S., and Todd, W.B. Oxford: Clarendon Press.

Thucydides (1954) *History of the Peloponnesian War.* Harmondsworth: Penguin.

Urry, J. (2000) *Sociology Beyond Societies: Mobilities for the Twenty-first Century.* London: Routledge.

Chapter 4

Public service motivation and ethos

Why do public officials work above and beyond the call of duty?

LEARNING OBJECTIVES

By the end of this chapter you should:

- understand the meaning and purpose of public service motivation
- be able to evaluate the similarities and differences between public service ethos and public service motivation concepts
- have examined some of the research evidence
- have considered the influences, rhetoric and reality of public service motivations in contemporary contexts
- be aware of methods of cultivating public service motivation.

KEY POINTS IN THIS CHAPTER

- Public service ethos and motivation is a dynamic phenomenon supported by a value system that differentiates that of the private sector.
- Public service ethos and motivations to work in the public sector can be measured and outcomes identified.
- The changing environment impacts public service ethos and motivations.
- There are positive associations with a public service ethos and motivation and, as such, these values and beliefs should be nurtured.

KEY TERMS

- **Public service ethos (PSE)** – characterized by a set of values such as honesty, integrity, accountability and probity and a set of processes involving, for example, recruitment and promotion on merit. It presupposes that those who subscribe to this ethos will be concerned to promote the public interest, rather than private interests.

- **Public service motivation (PSM)** – the belief, values and attitudes that go beyond self-interest and organizational interest and that motivate individuals to act accordingly whenever appropriate. As such, some individuals place a higher value on helping others and performing work that is considered worthwhile.

- **Public private partnerships (PPPs)** – describe a government service or private business venture which is funded and operated through a partnership of government and one or more private sector companies. These schemes involve a contract between a public sector authority and a private party, in which the private party provides a public service or project and assumes substantial financial, technical and operational risk in the project.

- **Organizational citizenship behaviour (OCB)** – perceived when individuals within organizations work beyond their formal contracts and/or take on work that is discretionary, not directly or explicitly recognized by the formal reward system. OCB helps promote the effective functioning of the organization as it can be described as a general tendency to be helpful and co-operative in organizational settings.

INTRODUCTION

A key aim of this chapter is to gain a greater understanding of public service motivation. In doing this we have considered some of the growing research around the subject and gained insight into the extent to which it is a universal concept. As this is a dynamic concept we have also identified factors that are likely to undermine or inhibit it, and we have provided suggestions as to how it can be cultivated. This chapter considers why individuals join the public services and continue to be committed to 'making a difference' to the lives of others and explains why some individuals are motivated to work in the public sector. In particular, it discusses the relationship between public service motivation and public service ethos and the associations of these concepts highlighting positive outcomes such as commitment, organizational citizenship behaviour and job satisfaction.

A critical factor in the delivery of public services has been an allegiance of professionals to an ethos of public service (Horton 2008). Whether the terms used are 'public service motivation' or 'public service ethos', what we are concerned with is the notion that individuals working in the public service generally have been identified as possessing somewhat different values, beliefs and motivations to those employed in the private sector. Values intrinsic to public service are said to include commitment, accountability, integrity, impartiality, organizational citizenship behaviour and some notion of the public interest, distinct from private interests. As such we look at the foundations and development of such notions taking both a UK and worldview perspective. We examine the research evidence relating to this phenomenon and consider the contemporary influences concerning its sustainability and possibly cultivation.

To illuminate the character of public service ethos and motivations we seek to answer some key questions.

- Why is it that individuals want to work in the public sector when similar jobs in other sectors might reward them more?
- How do public service employees deliver services in accordance with this ethos?
- What ends do they perceive it to endorse?
- Are public service values, beliefs and self-image changing?
- Does the organization appear to be deviating from public service ethos goals?
- Does an individual's integrity conflict with the organization's demands?
- Does the role of the public service employee still fit with the individual's in a new public management (NPM)/post-NPM environment?
- Can organizational leaders foster such an ethos and motivation?

We also address some of these questions in different ways in other chapters.

THE DEVELOPMENT OF PUBLIC SERVICE ETHOS AND MOTIVATION

A public service ethos began to emerge, in the UK, following the Northcote–Trevelyan report (1854) on the civil service. Numerous scholars have explored the ethos from a historical perspective and found its roots in the concept of public duty articulated in Plato and Aristotle and, more recently, the British idealists, notably T.H. Green (O'Toole 1993). The focus of these scholars is the senior civil service in the UK and the development of a public service ethos from the nineteenth-century civil service reforms onwards. A concern with ethical ideals, including service to the community, characterizes this development (Thomas 1989). Originally this ethos was adopted by an elite group of civil servants but ultimately it is recognized by a broad range of public sector workers.

It is claimed that individuals working in the public services are bound by, subscribe to, and motivated by a public service ethos (Vandenabeele, Scheepers and Hondeghem 2006). It is characterized by a set of values such as honesty, integrity, accountability and probity and a set of processes involving, for example, recruitment and promotion on merit. It presupposes that those who subscribe to this ethos will be concerned to promote the public interest, howsoever defined, rather than private interests (House of Commons Public Administration Select Committee 2002). The House of Commons report cited above endorsed the existence, and importance, of a public service ethos, defining it as

> a principled framework for action, something that describes the general character of an organization, but which, and more importantly should also motivate those who belong to it.
>
> (para 4: 7)

So, you may ask, what purpose does this ethos serve? Essentially, it describes an existing state of affairs, provides guidance for action and inspires those who work in public service organizations. The basis of public service ethos goes beyond these characterizations to suggest that public sector professionals are motivated to perform helping behaviours due to an intrinsic value system that includes altruistic behaviour as well as a belief in a 'public service ethos' (Le Grand 2003). The traditional view of this ethos 'emphasizes service, duty and obligation, rather than financial viability, profit or shareholder value' (Audit Commission 2002: 58). It has subsequently been defined as

> a way of life that includes a set of values held by the individual, together with organizational processes and procedures that shape, and are shaped by, those values. Such values are enshrined in organizational goals that are directed towards public rather than private or sectional interests.
>
> (Rayner *et al.* 2011: 29)

DISTINGUISHING PUBLIC SERVICE ETHOS FROM PUBLIC SERVICE MOTIVATION

Having established what is meant by a public service ethos, we find that it is highly similar to the public service motivation construct, and this is evidenced by the terms often being used interchangeably. Indeed, both can be described as umbrella terms based on the premise that some individuals are highly attracted and motivated by public service work. Public service motivation is most recently defined as 'the belief, values and attitudes that go beyond self-interest and organizational interest, that concern the interest of a larger political entity and that motivate individuals to act accordingly whenever appropriate' (Vandenabeele 2007: 547). As such it is claimed that some individuals place a higher value on helping others and performing work that is worthwhile (Crewson 1997; Grant 2007). Public service motivation is therefore located in individuals regardless of their context, rather than being an ethos that is sector-based. Either way, research shows that people involved in public services derive job satisfaction and describe their attitudes towards it in terms of 'making a difference'.

Indeed, there has been a wealth of research on public service motivation and evidence that individuals who choose a career in the public service are different from those who choose the private sector. For example, it has been argued that public sector employees are more altruistic and pro-socially oriented than those employed in the private sector (Hebson, Grimshaw and Marchington 2003), although to what extent this can be explained by a public service ethos rather than, for example, personality factors, age or gender has not been established. To date, attempts to measure the relationship of this ethos towards such outcomes as commitment and organizational citizenship behaviour (OCB) is lacking. In contrast, the related construct 'public service motivation' (PSM) has been building internationally for over 20 years assisted by the development of a tool to measure this phenomenon (see Perry 1996). More recently this had been used to identify its relationship to work outcomes such as commitment and organizational citizenship. It is also argued that public employees are motivated by a sense of service not generally found among business employees (see Vandenabeele and Van de Walle 2008; Perry and Hondeghem 2008). The questions raised are, what exactly is meant by public service motivation and public service ethos? How similar are these two constructs, should we use them interchangeably and if not, how do we distinguish between them and how do they relate to each other? We discuss these issues below.

THE BASIS OF PUBLIC SERVICE MOTIVATION AS DISTINCT FROM PUBLIC SERVICE ETHOS

It is recognized that both public service motivation and public service ethos are dynamic constructs and as such present difficulties for measurement. Unlike the traditional and philosophical roots of public service ethos the bases of public service motivation are founded in motivation theory and derived from three types of motives: affective, normative and rational (Perry and Wise 1990; Brewer, Selden and Facer 2000). From the affective dimension it is claimed that individuals are attracted to public service through emotional attachments such as a conviction about the importance of a particular public service. For example, why do some people choose to enter nursing, police forces and social services? It is generally not due to attractive salaries or working conditions. The normative perspective suggests the attraction is based on ethical reasons such as equity and fairness. Hence, you may be able to think of people who have entered local politics or who work with boards of governance in schools, colleges and community initiatives in an attempt to bring about such equity and fairness to citizens. The rational perspective suggests the basis is aligned to self-interest, leading individuals to be attracted to policy-making to promote such an interest. This departs from the traditional public

---

BOX 4.1 EX-MPs FACE BAN

Three former MPs could be banned from entering parliament after they were found to have broken Commons rules on lobbying and offering political influence for money . . .

A group of journalists set up a bogus lobbying company and offered to pay the three in return for access to government. All three left parliament at the general election but kept their Westminster passes.

Source: *Sunday Times* (2011)

---

service ethos construct in a fundamental way: namely, public service ethos (as understood in the previous section) relates to the character of an organization and espouses aspirational and normative ideologies that are intended to bind and motivate those who belong to such organizations. Of course, there are myriad examples of public servants who do not live up to such ideals, or worse, who use their power and position of trust to abuse the system as illustrated in Box 4.1.

Notwithstanding this, it is argued that the values of public sector workers differentiate them from others. People may choose to be doctors, teachers or social workers based on all sorts of motivations although employment is more often located in the public, rather than private, sector. Research conducted by the Audit Commission (2002: 16) found 'choice of career would be based on the specific characteristics of the job – no one said they were committed to working in the public sector per se'. Moreover:

> The biggest single reason that people identify for joining the public sector is the opportunity to 'make a difference' for service users and local communities. People want to 'make a difference' in a job that satisfies them, and with a reward package that meets their needs. Taken together, these three factors need to outweigh the alternatives that are open to them. And, for most people, sector is not a deciding factor – they choose a job or profession, not a sector.
>
> (Audit Commission 2002: 13)

Consider Exercise 4.1, which shows a public servant who does not epitomize the general attitudes and behaviour associated with public service.

Discussion questions

- What are the key issues and motivations implicit in this case?
- Should employees in such public service departments have the right to use Twitter during work hours?

EXERCISE 4.1   CIVIL SERVANT TWEETS 100 TIMES A WEEK AT WORK

A senior government official fears she will lose her job after warning on her blog that coalition cuts will leave Britain with a 'Tesco Civil Service'.

In an apparent break of impartiality rules, Sarah Baskerville, a team manager at the Department for Transport (DfT) accused politicians who have criticized the civil service of 'bullying and harassment' and has warned that their attacks were leaving Whitehall feeling demoralized.

She is also a prolific user of Twitter and has sent thousands of messages over the past three years on the minutiae of her daily life. In the past two weeks she appears to have posted more than 200 tweets during office hours, complaining in one that she is 'struggling with a red wine induced headache'.

Baskerville also describes the growing scrutiny Whitehall is under as follows:

'I'm spending more and more of my time filling out HR justification forms, business cases . . . to justify keeping my team together – a whole cottage industry has sprung up requiring more resources.'

At times her tweets appear overtly political. During a recent management course she promoted an attack by Tom Watson, the Labour MP, on Downing Street spin. In another tweet she asked, 'How much more can we take from this Government? Seriously?'

Baskerville claimed her use of Twitter was within civil service rules. She said, 'The Cabinet Office clearly states that "Yes, you can use Twitter".' She added that she had been 'totally overwhelmed' by the criticism levelled at her.

On Twitter she was more vocal, posting five tweets about her exposure in an hour. 'Bit upset . . . bit bewildered . . . no idea what I have done to deserve this', she wrote.

The DfT said, 'We expect all civil servants to abide by the civil service code.'

Source: Swinford (2011)

- How would you distinguish between legitimate and illegitimate use of e-mail and social networking sights during work hours?
- How can we distinguish between public service employees' freedom of speech, whistle-blowing, and claims of 'bullying and harassment'?
- Should public service employees exhibit independent judgement/behaviour?
- How would you manage Sarah Baskerville?

Commentary

In answering these questions you might like to think about some of the following points. Identify the fundamental causes of Sarah's dissatisfaction and frustration in the way she perceives her work. These are causing her to vent her anger. However, is it appropriate for employees in such organizations to participate in social networking sites during work hours? Could this be interpreted as dishonest behaviour (i.e. using work time for personal purposes)? Is it acceptable to communicate dissent of this nature about any employing organization outside of work hours and if so is it more unacceptable when the source is a public servant? Alternatively, could this be a healthy exercise aligned to freedom of speech or disloyal and destructive activity that may impact commitment and damage the organization's image, sense of purpose and unity towards public service? Is there a written, implicit or psychological contract in place that communicates the standards of 'tweeting' and cultural acceptance of such behaviours and use of other electronic means and social networking sites?

RESEARCH EVIDENCE

Research identifying the essence of public service ethos confirms four key ideas: first, that a public service ethos exists; second, that there is something distinctive about it; third, that professionals who work in the public, rather than private sector have a belief system that motivates them by something different; and finally, that working for the public interest is an important feature of this ethos. Therefore, it is multi-dimensional and it may be helpful to try to delineate the dimensions of public service ethos:

> Public Service Belief encapsulates why individuals are motivated to work for the public services and reflects personal attributes such as altruism, compassion and sentiments of wanting to make a difference to the lives of others.

> Public Service Practice is concerned with how organizational values, processes and practices including accountability, fairness and probity are perceived to support motivation towards public service.

> Public Interest reflects the ends of public office such that individuals act in the interests of the common good rather than in their own selfish interests, the interest of particular groups or other individuals.

> (Rayner et al. 2011a: 30)

With these definitions and dimensions in mind we can consider how this ethos relates to public service motivation and impacts both the individual and the organizational level. Work by Perry and Vandenabeele (2008) presents a motivation framework that operates at both these levels. Similarly, developments in the public service motivation literature have explored the value congruence between the individual and the organization (Moynihan and Pandey 2007; Paarlberg and Perry 2007; Wright and Pandey 2008). We argue that the public service ethos framework provides a 'fit' not only between individual and organizational values, but also with societal values.

> First, a belief in public service underpins **why** individuals might align themselves to an ethos which puts public interests before private interests and goes beyond exchange theory explanations of motivation (see Blau 1964). Second, a recognizable set of norms concerning public service practice which is indicative of **how**, ideally, individuals within public sector organizations should behave. Third, a central value of working in the public interest which explains to **what ends** this ethos serves. So, having discussed why individuals want to work in the public sector, how they deliver services in accordance to a public service ethos and the ends it endorses we need to consider whether public service values, belief and self image are changing
>
> (Rayner *et al.* 2011a:31)

Research has shown that there are a range of antecedents that have some bearing on levels of public service motivations. For example, socio-demographic factors such as older individuals, education, and females rather than males have all been found to be antecedents that may lead to higher levels of public service motivation. These can be explained in terms of older members in organizations being able to influence policy, females as possessing caring, altruistic and nurturing qualities, and education as shaping ideological beliefs (in particular, teaching practical citizenship and highlighting the relationship between the individual and the community). Family can also be influential in terms of parental modelling as can a particular profession which espouses an ethical code of behaviour. There are also correlates associated with public service ethos and motivations.

Interestingly, there is a dearth of research evidence pertaining to public service ethos, a situation that contrasts with public service motivation research. For example, over the last decade alone, a considerable body of empirical evidence has demonstrated that public service motivation is associated with forms of self-sacrifice such as whistle-blowing; is positively related to high performance, job satisfaction and commitment; places less value on extrinsic reward motivators such as high income and short work hours and more value on altruistic behaviour and public service activity; and is predictive of organizational citizenship behaviour and decreased tendency to leave the job (e.g. Pandey, Wright and Moynihan 2008; Perry, Hondeghem and Wise 2010). Although studies have been predominantly conducted in the US, more recently research has emerged from Europe (e.g. Vandenabeele 2009; Ritz 2009), Asia (e.g. Choi 2004; Kim 2006, 2009a and b) and Australia (Taylor 2007, 2008).

Such research shows that public service motivation is positively related to a range of desirable organizational attitudes and behaviours, and therefore supports claims that it has substantial organizational and social significance (e.g. Pandey and Stazyk 2008). In comparison, empirical evidence measuring public service ethos is nascent.

THE CHANGING ENVIRONMENT: A CONTEMPORARY VIEW

Rightly or wrongly, in the past, public service ethos was considered unique to the public sector and did not extend to the beliefs and types of behaviour exhibited by individuals outside such contexts. Arguably, following NPM, this ethos, or parts of it, may be apparent in individuals working to deliver public services outside the traditional public sector as evidenced by the House of Commons Public Administration Select Committee (2002): 'We conclude that, in the mixed economy of public service, it is possible for private and voluntary sector bodies and people to uphold the public service ethos, however, the profit motive may put it under strain' (para 32: 13).

Clearly, reforms to, and contextual changes for, the public sector under the guise of NPM, well documented elsewhere, have encouraged the adoption of private sector management values and principles (Pollitt and Bouckaert 2000; Maesschalck, Van der Wal and Huberts 2008). These new values derive, in part, from recognition of market forces and customer sovereignty, which, it is argued, is antithetical to a commitment to the public interest (Hebson *et al.* 2003). These values include profitability, risk-taking, responsiveness, innovation and enterprise (Van der Wal, de Graaf and Lasthuizen 2008). The literature indicates that, on the whole, these reforms have altered roles (Bach, Kessler and Heron 2007), influenced norms, and significantly and negatively affected public service professionals and the public service ethos. Outcomes that have been cited include the undermining of professional values, the lowering of morale, motivation, trust, commitment and job satisfaction (Foster and Wilding 2000), and increasing stress through work intensification (Exworthy and Halford 1999). These experiences can be generalized throughout the public sector both in the UK and internationally as professionals in, for example, health, education, the civil service and social work have been subject to similar reforms (Frederickson and Ghere 2005). Clearly, there is evidence that NPM reforms have impacted public service ethos and motivation generally through the creation of an audit culture and specifically in the areas of public private partnerships (PPPs) and in contracting out. Such claims have led to a renewed interest in the public service ethos and to attempts to sharpen its focus in responding to such reforms (Needham 2006). Now read Box 4.2 and consider the discussion questions that follow.

BOX 4.2 FROM DUTY OF CARE TO MARKET FORCES

The case of Stafford Hospital, where 400 patients may have died because of poor care.

The Healthcare Commission's chairman, Sir Ian Kennedy, describes it as a story of 'appalling standards of care and chaotic systems for looking after patients . . . There were inadequacies at every stage.' The patients died at a time when the hospital was trying to achieve foundation status, which would signify that it was rated as one of the leading NHS hospitals in the UK.

'A hospital is able to tick all the boxes, yet still utterly fail patients.' How did we get into this situation? Well, the Stafford problems can be traced back to the reforms of the Conservative government in the early 1980s, and the obsession with market forces as an unlimited good. At that time, the health service was in need of reform; it needed to be brought up to date. But the desire to find better ways to manage the day-to-day running of the hospital morphed into a perception that clinical staff – doctors in particular – needed kicking into gear. There was this assumption that came with it, that doctors – and nurses – could not be relied upon to drive clinical efficiency on their own, through sheer professionalism and pride in their work.

When the NHS was set up, it was an egalitarian system 'free at the point of access, independent of the ability to pay'. Recently, there have been much repeated anecdotes featuring consultants down at the golf course or working in the private sector on NHS time – and while those people probably existed, they were a tiny minority. The vast majority of doctors were out there doing far more than their fair share of work, because they believed in the delivery of good service in the best interest of their patients. Unfortunately, no one could measure goodwill or professionalism.

So we went from a system driven by professional pride and duty of care to one that would accommodate market forces.

Source: Green (2009)

Discussion questions

- Ethics are standards and values that people use to judge what is right, good or worthwhile; they set the maximum or ideal standards the profession should aspire to. Identify and discuss the unintended consequences of reform in the Stafford Hospital case.
- Evaluate the statement 'managing public sector organizations from a market forces perspective is a good thing'.

■ How could public service ethos be fostered in such an environment as Stafford Hospital? (Table 4.2 will help here.)

Commentary

Consider the political pressures on the hospital to demonstrate efficiency and effectiveness and the difficulties in measuring elements of patient care. What should be measured? What cannot be measured? How useful are league tables? Chapter 8 on ethical performance management will provide greater insight here.

It is also important to bear in mind that professionals historically have engendered an understanding with society that they espouse certain values and uphold a code of ethics that puts public interest ahead of personal interest. In evaluating market forces in this context you need to consider the egalitarian nature of the UK's National Health Service and the ideological conflicts inherent in responding to market forces and what it means to the health professionals in terms of autonomy and use of their professional judgement. At the same time, resources are limited, so you need to reflect on how health professionals can manage these tensions. Consider the main philosophical approaches commonly associated with ethical decision-making:

Consequentialism – what makes an action right or wrong is the consequence/ outcome of that action.
Deontology – some human actions are intrinsically right or wrong (based on Divine Law or universalism), irrespective of their consequences.

The basic principles here are 'do unto others', that is, never behave in ways or treat others in ways that you would not like to be treated yourself.

CHANGE IN THE PUBLIC SECTOR

The following quote encapsulates areas of concern expressed by early commentators on the changes experienced by public sector professionals:

> If they, professionals, are to be mere passive employees without a strong organized voice in the allocation of the resources which are essential for doing good work, they will find it difficult to remain committed to doing good work. If they are to play the role of merely providing whatever is demanded by consumers and authorized by those who pay for it, they will find it difficult to preserve a sense of the value of their schooled judgement. If they are to be merely loyal servants of the interests of their employers or their own 'business', they will have difficulty in sustaining any independent commitment to serving the good of both individual clients and the public. And if they are to be

required to work within ultimately mechanical, albeit permissive, standards established and enforced by professionals who act as their administrative and cognitive superiors, they will have to forsake the communal and collegiate principle that is distinctive of the professional mode of organizing work.

(Friedson 1994: 215)

In a work context, the management literature claims, in general, that commitment is engendered primarily by managers. We believe that the issue of commitment transcends the managerial agenda and that commitments made by individuals represent the values and beliefs they hold and the priorities they choose and actions they take over long periods of their lives. Although 'social' values are important to both public and private sector employees, it is argued that they are more important to those in the public sector. Therefore, is this ethos and public service motivation portable to organizations outside of this sector that are working towards delivering efficient and effective public services? For example, public services are increasingly delivered through networks of public, private and third sector organizations (see Thomson, Perry and Miller 2007). One fear is that professionals working in these organizations will not identify with traditional values attached to public sector behaviour. See Table 4.1 on the following page, which provides current impressions of how public servants feel about their work. This data is from a survey conducted for the Australian Public Service Commission.

The question to ask is: how is the current environment impacting some of the outcomes traditionally associated with public service ethos and motivation? In this chapter we have mentioned a range of positive outcomes shown to be related to these constructs and now focus on one outcome in particular: organizational citizenship behaviour (OCB). We believe this to be of importance in public service not only because of its associations with public service ethos but also for the reason it can enhance the relationship between citizens and public servants. As such OCB is of commercial value, having been found to improve competitiveness and promote effective functioning of the organization through behaviour that managers want but cannot demand. It is also an area that we feel is in danger of being undermined or eroded following NPM and post-NPM reform (Rayner, Lawton and Williams 2011).

Some critics argue that the impact of such reforms crowd out traditional values (Moynihan 2008). Crowding out is a useful theory offering an explanation of the adverse impact of externally generated reforms, such as those associated with NPM. In a world of market forces and limited resources, how can managers of public sector organizations cultivate, as opposed to 'crowd out', such behaviours? Perhaps the most comprehensive explanation of the effect of OCB can be located in self-determination theory. Here activities can be undertaken due to an inner incentive that requires no external pressure as it is intrinsically motivated (e.g. public good; a belief in public service and the public interest). Alternatively, they

61

Table 4.1 *State of Service Employee Survey Results 2008–9*

General Impressions: 2009

Please rate your level of agreement with the following statements regarding your current job:	Strongly Agree %	Agree %	Neither agree nor disagree %	Disagree %	Strongly disagree %	Not sure %
a. I enjoy the work in my current job	19	62	12	6	2	0
b. I am motivated to do the best possible work that I can	33	52	10	5	1	0
c. When needed I am willing to put in the extra effort to get the job done	53	44	2	1	0	0
d. My job allows me to utilize my skills, knowledge and abilities	20	54	12	10	3	0
e. My current job will help my career aspirations	12	37	32	14	5	1
f. My job gives me a feeling of personal accomplishment	16	51	19	11	3	0
g. I have a clear understanding of how my own job contributes to my work team's role	34	56	7	2	1	0
h. I clearly understand what is expected of me in this job	31	54	9	4	1	0
i. I have the authority (e.g. the necessary delegation(s), autonomy, level of responsibility) to do my job effectively	18	59	13	8	2	0
j. I receive adequate feedback on my performance to enable me to deliver required results	14	53	17	12	4	0
k. I am satisfied with the recognition I receive for doing a good job	12	42	22	17	6	0
l. I am fairly remunerated for the work that I do	12	51	19	13	5	0
m. I understand how my agency's decision-making processes operate (e.g. relevant committee structures and how committees are linked)	11	56	20	9	3	1
n. I have the skills to negotiate conflict with others	17	65	13	4	0	0
o. The work I do requires an understanding of national and international trends	16	42	24	13	3	2

Source: Australian Public Services Commission (2009)

may be the result of external incentives and require external pressure (e.g. rewards and targets). Rewards that are contingent on performance are mostly perceived as reducing self-determination. This is explained by Weibel, Rost and Osterloh (2007) as having two underlying mechanisms: either actors accept and pursue market incentives as a means to keep their job, or they get disillusioned with it as it 'devaluates the sense of inherent value of the work they and their colleagues undertake' (Moynihan 2008: 251). The following quote from a survey of lecturers in the England underpins this notion:

> With the current climate of cuts in Adult Education in colleges, I am actively planning to leave my post within the next 12 months. I am strongly opposed to the Government's directives and my college's interpretation of them, and I am not going to 'manage' the demise of Adult Education in my community.
> (Reported in Rayner 2007: 194)

Given NPM reform and the subsequent contextual changes in the way in which public sector organizations are managed and funded, it has been theorized that OCB directed towards the organization may be inhibited and 'crowded out'. For example, the time individuals allocate to OCB may be at the expense of task performance, and such extra role behaviours may have a detrimental impact on individuals in terms of limiting rewards (Bergeron 2007). This raises the question as to whether OCB directed towards the organization is discouraged unintentionally by reforms. If yes, then this can be credited to a value system that, for example, encourages professionals to satisfy targets by which they are measured, rather than participate in helpful behaviours towards the organization as this may not be recognized formally in any reward system.

We believe public sector organizations themselves have an important role in preventing the erosion of the public service ethos as well as shaping and cultivating it. However, this may be more easily said than done given the claim that the NPM value system is incongruent with parts of the 'traditional' public service ethos (Vigoda and Golembiewski 2001). As with most public sector organizations, NPM has fundamentally changed the basis of organizational design, control and reward both in the UK and internationally.

The financial constraints and increasing controls set by such bodies result in increased stress and work intensification for professionals. Further, insufficient funds often produce tensions between competition and collegiality (Fitzgerald and Ferlie 2000). Some commentators suggest this leads to neglect of other community interests such as adult education at the expense of vocational education.

Consider the following quote from a survey of lecturers in England:

> I do this part-time teaching for fun not for money. I teach adult learners professional qualifications. I feel I am putting something back into society.

I enjoy working with adults and value what they teach me! I have little loyalty to the college but loads for the students.

(reported in Rayner 2007: 190)

In applying exchange theory, employees with high job congruence will more likely perceive their employing organization as fair and reciprocate with OCB towards it. It also suggests why the adoption of 'alien' values may lead to some professionals feeling disinclined to exhibit OCB towards the organization and, again, may crowd out public service-related behaviour due to an overemphasis on extrinsic motivations rather than intrinsic motivations such as, for example, a belief in public service. For a full discussion of this see Rayner *et al.* (2011b).

Consider Exercise 4.2.

EXERCISE 4.2   NURSES TO MARCH TO VICTORIA PARLIAMENT OVER PAY

Sydney Morning Herald, 23 November 2011

A sea of red will surge towards Parliament House in Melbourne at lunchtime on Thursday as nurses march for better pay and conditions after making little progress in negotiations. Nurses, their supporters and members of other unions plan to begin marching at 12.30pm (AEDT) from the Bourke Street Mall to parliament wearing their red campaign t-shirts.

'We think it's very important to give the community an opportunity to show their support for the nurses – we've had a lot of people phoning in and saying they want to come,' Ms Fitzpatrick said.

Health Minister David Davis said nurses had picketed a number of offices on Wednesday, including his. Three nurses had set up a card table there and were offered tea and coffee by his staff. 'Nurses want improved nurse-to-patient ratios and a pay rise of 18.5 per cent over three years and eight months.' The government wants to have flexibility in the ratios and has offered a wage increase of 2.5 per cent plus productivity improvements.

Discussion questions

- Is the primary concern of these nurses the welfare of patients or pay?
- Given that at the time of action the global economy is concerned with recession and world debt, is it appropriate for nurses to take such action?

- How would you resolve this situation so as to prevent industrial action and ensure a fair outcome to all?
- Is this possible and, if not, where should compromises be directed?

Commentary

Arguably, their public service motivation is apparent in this case if nurses are willing to have wages docked to protect the conditions of patients. Or, do you take the view that self-interest in terms of pay is the motivator?

TIME TO REFLECT: CULTIVATING PUBLIC SERVICE VALUES AND BELIEFS

As discussed earlier, individuals' feelings of making a difference in public service can manifest in outcomes such as commitment, OCB and job satisfaction, to name a few. Therefore, how can we harness it? There are some excellent suggestions from Paarlberg, Perry and Hondeghem (2008) concerning recruitment and selection of those with strong intrinsic motivations to serve the public good. For example, ensure person and organization fit by promoting public service values and selecting individuals who are responsive to such values. Situational judgement tests may assist here as they present challenging and realistic situations people may encounter in the job and ask them, 'What might you do in this situation?' Table 4.2 on the following page presents tactics to be adopted.

CONCLUSIONS

To summarize, this chapter has discussed public service values and beliefs and has identified the difference between public service motivation as being located in individuals regardless of their context, and public service ethos which is sector-based and explicitly requires supporting organizational processes and values. It has illuminated the relationship between the two concepts and provided a brief critique of the empirical evidence concerning these phenomena. We have presented a range of empirical evidence of positive outcomes resulting from the adoption of public service ethos beliefs and values and in particular the importance of OCB in relationship to these. You have been encouraged to think about the changing environment and how it might impact public service values, beliefs and motivations. Contemporary factors affecting the alignment of these have been highlighted together with the unintended consequences of some reforms resulting in, for example, the crowding out of OCB. As to whether this public service ethos and motivation is changing or eroding, the question can only be answered with more certainty via longitudinal measurement. This would assist in gathering empirical data that supports or refutes claims as well as measuring the strength of public service ethos across different public service contexts.

Table 4.2 *Tactics to be adopted*

Strategy	Tactic	Description
Integrate public service ethos and motivation into HRM processes	1	Use public service motivation as a selection criterion for entry into organization.
	2	Provide formal and informal opportunities for newcomers to learn about organizational values and expectations for employee behaviour that reflect public service values.
	3	Develop performance appraisals and performance monitoring systems that include observations of behaviours that reflect and encourage public service ethos and motivation.
Create and convey meaning and purpose in the job	4	Identify beneficiaries of jobs; establish opportunities for direct contact between employee and beneficiary; and provide clear channels for service beneficiary feedback.
	5	Interpret broad public service missions in terms of clear and meaningful work expectations.
Create a supportive work environment for public service ethos and motivation	6	Develop work structures that enhance self-regulation through empowerment and participatory decision-making.
	7	Commit to creating a supportive workplace environment that models and reinforces public service ethos and motivation.
Integrate public service into organization mission and strategy	8	Create and maintain incentives that align organizational mission and employee predispositions.
	9	Design compensation systems to emphasize long-term attractiveness to employees and avoid performance-related pay that might crowd out intrinsic motivations.
	10	Articulate and symbolize organization mission and vision in ways that connect with employees' zone of existing public service values.
	11	Encourage and reward the development of leaders who communicate and model public service ethos and motivation.
Create societal legitimacy for public service	12	Foster institutional support for incorporation of public service values into professional and educational curriculum.
	13	Advocate for and provide opportunities for pre-service experiences.
	14	Bring public service to the attention of the broader society.

Adapted from Paarlberg *et al.* (2008: 270–86)

In the meantime, we propose that managers, individuals and organizations have a role to play in cultivating public service values, beliefs and motivations given the myriad claims that it is to be nurtured and cherished, together with concerns regarding its erosion. The importance of managers taking responsibility to not only support and sustain such motivations and ethos but also to engender value congruence between the individual and the organization has been emphasized.

REFERENCES

Audit Commission (2002) *Recruitment and Retention: Public Sector National Report.* London: Audit Commission.

Australian Public Services Commission (2009) *State of Service Employee Survey Results 2008–9.* Canberra: Australian Government.

Bach, S., Kessler, I. and Heron, P. (2007) 'The Consequences of Assistant Roles in the Public Services: Degradation or Empowerment?', *Human Relations* 60 (9): 1267–92.

Bergeron, D.M. (2007) 'The Potential Paradox of Organizational Citizenship Behavior: Good Citizens at What Cost?', *Academy of Management Review* 32 (4): 1078–95.

Blau, P.M. (1964) *Exchange and Power in Social Life.* New York: John Wiley and Sons.

Brewer, G.A. and Selden, S.C. (1998) 'Whistle Blowers in the Federal Civil Service: New Evidence of the Public Service Ethic', *Journal of Public Administration Research and Theory* 8 (3): 413–40.

Brewer, G.A., Selden, S.C. and Facer, II R.L. (2000) 'Individual Conceptions of Public Service Motivation', *Public Administration Review* 60 (3): 254–65.

Choi, D.L. (2004) 'Public Service Motivation and Ethical Conduct', *International Journal of Public Administration* 8 (2): 99–106.

Crewson, P.E. (1997) 'Public Service Motivation: Building Empirical Evidence of Incidence and Effect', *Journal of Public Administration Research and Theory* 7 (4): 499–518.

Exworthy, M. and Halford, S. (eds) (1999) *Professionals and the New Managerialism.* Buckingham: Open University Press.

Fitzgerald, L. and Ferlie, E. (2000) 'Professionals: Back to the Future', *Human Relations* 53 (5): 713–39.

Foster, P. and Wilding, P. (2000) 'Whither Welfare Professionalism?', *Social Policy and Administration* 34 (2): 143–59.

Frederickson, G.H. and Ghere, R.K. (2005) *Ethics in the Public Management Sector.* New York: M.E. Sharpe.

Friedson, E. (1994) *Professionalism Reborn.* Cambridge: Polity Press.

Grant, A.M. (2007) 'Employees Without a Cause: The Motivational Effects of Prosocial Impact in Public Service', *International Public Management Journal* 11 (1): 48–66.

Green, P. (2009) 'A Hospital is Able to Tick All the Boxes, Yet Still Utterly Fail Patients', *Guardian*, 19 March.

Hebson, G., Grimshaw, D. and Marchington, M. (2003) 'PPPs and the Changing Public Sector Ethos: Case Study Evidence from the Health and Local Authority Sectors', *Work, Employment and Society* 69 (3): 481–501.

Horton, S. (2008) 'History and Persistence of an Ideal' in Perry, J.L. and Hondeghem, A. (eds) *Motivation in Public Management: The Call of Public Service*. Oxford: Oxford University Press, pp. 17–32.

House of Commons Public Administration Select Committee (2002) *Seventh Report: The Public Service Ethos*. London: HMSO.

Kim, S. (2006) 'Public Service Motivation and Organizational Citizenship Behavior in Korea', *International Journal of Manpower* 27 (8): 722–40.

Kim, S. (2009a) 'Revising Perry's Measurement Scale of Public Service Motivation', *The American Review of Public Administration* 39 (2): 149–61.

Kim, S. (2009b) 'Testing the Structure of Public Service Motivation in Korea: A Research Note', *Journal of Public Administration Research and Theory* 19 (4): 839–51.

Le Grand, J. (2003) *Motivation, Agency and Public Policy: Of Knights and Knaves, Pawns and Queens*. Oxford: Oxford University Press.

Maesschalck, J., Van der Wal, Z. and Huberts, L. (2008) 'Public Service Motivation and Ethical Conduct' in Perry, J.L. and Hondeghem, A. (eds) *Motivation in Public Management: The Call of Public Service*. Oxford: Oxford University Press, pp. 157–76.

Moynihan, D.P. (2008) 'The Normative Model in Decline? Public Service Motivation in the Age of Governance' in Perry, J.L. and Hondeghem, A. (eds) *Motivation in Public Management: The Call of Public Service*. Oxford: Oxford University Press, pp. 247–67.

Moynihan, D.P. and Pandey, S.K. (2007) 'The Role of Organizations in Fostering Public Service Motivation', *Public Administration Review* 67 (1): 40–53.

Needham, C. (2006) 'Customer Care and Public Service Ethos', *Public Administration* 84 (4): 845–60.

Northcote, S. and Trevelyan, C. (1854) *Report on the Organisation of the Permanent Civil Service*. C1713 Copy as Appendix 1 of Fulton Report (1968). The Civil Service, Vol. 1, Report of the Committee Cmnd. 3638 London: HMSO.

O'Toole, B. (1993) 'The Loss of Purity: The Corruption of Public Service in Britain', *Public Policy and Administration* 8 (2): 1–6.

Paarlberg, L. and Perry, J.L. (2007) 'Values Management Aligning Employee Values and Organization Goals', *The American Review of Public Administration* 37 (4): 387–408.

Paarlberg, L., Perry, J.L. and Hondeghem, A. (2008) 'From Theory to Practice: Strategies for Applying Public Service Motivation' in Perry, J.L. and Hondeghem, A. (eds) *Motivation in Public Management: The Call of Public Service*. Oxford: Oxford University Press, pp. 268–93.

Pandey, S.K. and Stazyk, E.C. (2008) 'Antecedents and Correlates of Public Service Motivation' in Perry, J.L. and Hondeghem, A. (eds) *Motivation in Public Management: The Call of Public Service*. Oxford: Oxford University Press, pp. 101–17.

Pandey, S.K., Wright, B.E. and Moynihan, D.P. (2008) 'Public Service Motivation and Interpersonal Citizenship Behavior in Public Organizations: Testing a Preliminary Model', *International Public Management Journal* 11 (1): 89–108.

Perry, J.L. (1996) 'Measuring Public Service Motivation: An Assessment of Construct Reliability and Validity', *Journal of Public Administration Research and Theory* 6 (1): 5–22.

Perry, J.L. and Hondeghem, A. (eds) (2008) *Motivation in Public Management: The Call of Public* Service. Oxford: Oxford University Press.

Perry, J.L. and Vandenabeele, W. (2008) 'Behavioral Dynamics: Institutions, Identities and Self-Regulation' Perry, J.L. and Hondeghem, A. (eds) *Motivation in Public Management: The Call of Public Service*. Oxford: Oxford University Press, pp. 56–79.

Perry, J.L. and Wise, L.R. (1990) 'The Motivational Bases of Public Service', *Public Administration Review* 50 (3): 367–73.

Perry, J.L., Hondeghem, A. and Wise, L.R. (2010) 'Revisiting the Motivational Bases of Public Service: Twenty Years of Research and an Agenda for the Future', *Public Administration Review* 70 (5): 681–90.

Pollitt, C. and Bouckaert, G. (2000) *Public Management Reform: A Comparative Analysis*. Oxford: Oxford University Press.

Rayner, J. (2007) *Ethos, Values and Commitment: Developments in the Further Education Sector – Developing Psychometric Instruments to Measure Attitudes and Beliefs*. Unpublished thesis.

Rayner, J., Lawton, A. and Williams, H.M. (2011b) 'Organizational Citizenship Behavior and the Public Service Ethos: Whither the Organization?' *Journal of Business Ethics* 106 (2): 117–30.

Rayner, J., Williams, H.M., Lawton, A. and Allinson, C.W. (2011a) 'Public Service Ethos: The Development of a Generic Measure', *Journal of Public Administration Research and Theory* 21 (1): 27–51.

Ritz, A. (2009) 'Public Service Motivation and Organizational Performance in Swiss Federal Government', *International Review of Administrative Sciences* 75 (1): 53–78.

Swinford, S. (2011) 'Civil Servant Tweets 100 Times a Week at Work', *Sunday Times*, 9 January.

Taylor, J. (2007) 'The Impact of Public Service Motives on Work Outcomes in Australia: A Comparative Multi-Dimensional Analysis', *Public Administration* 85 (4): 931–59.

—— (2008) 'Organizational Influences, Public Service Motivation and Work Outcomes: An Australian Study', *International Public Management Journal* 11(1): 67–88.

Thomas, R. (1989) *The British Philosophy of Administration: A comparison of British and American Ideas 1900–1939.* Cambridge: Centre for Business and Public Sector Ethics.

Thomson, A.M., Perry, J.L. and Miller, T.K. (2007) 'Conceptualizing and Measuring Collaboration', *Journal of Public Administration Research and Theory* 19 (1): 23–56.

Vandenabeele, W. (2007) 'Toward a Public Administration Theory of Public Service Motivation: An Institutional Approach', *Public Administration Review* 9 (4): 545–56.

—— (2009) 'The Mediating Effect of Job Satisfaction and Organizational Commitment on Self-Reported Performance: More Robust Evidence of PSM Performance Relationship', *International Review of Administrative Sciences* 75 (1): 11–34.

Vandenabeele, W. and Van de Walle, S. (2008) 'International Differences in Public Service Motivation' in Perry, J.L. and Hondeghem, A. (eds) *Motivation in Public Management: The Call of Public Service.* Oxford: Oxford University Press, pp. 223–46.

Vandenabeele, W., Scheepers, S. and Hondeghem, A. (2006) 'Public Service Motivation in an International Comparative Perspective: The UK and Germany', *Public Policy and Administration* 21 (1): 13–31.

Van der Wal, Z., de Graaf, G. and Lasthuizen, K. (2008) 'What's Valued Most? Similarities and Differences Between the Organizational Values of the Public and Private Sector', *Public Administration* 86 (2): 465–82.

Vigoda, E. and Golembiewski, R.T. (2001) 'Citizenship Behavior and the Spirit of New Managerialism: A Theoretical Framework and Challenge for Governance', *American Review of Public Administration* 31 (3): 273–95.

Weibel, A., Rost, K. and Osterloh, M. (2007) 'Crowding-out of Intrinsic Motivation: Opening the Black Box', *Social Science Research Network.* Retrieved from http://papers.ssrn.com/sol3/papers.cfm?abstract_id = 957770 (10 May 2007).

Wright, B.E. and Pandey, S. (2008) 'Public Service Motivation and the Assumption of Person-Organization Fit', *Administration and Society* 49 (5): 502–21.

Chapter 5

Ethical culture

What is it, is it universal and how can it be changed?

LEARNING OBJECTIVES

By the end of this chapter you should:

- understand what constitutes ethical culture
- have analyzed the factors that might influence ethical culture
- be able to demonstrate understanding and application of theoretical frameworks of culture
- appreciate the challenges involved in changing culture.

KEY POINTS IN THIS CHAPTER

- Given the extent of globalization, the influence of culture on ethical behaviour is an increasingly important issue.
- We can expect different interpretations of an ethical culture depending on the national/international cultural contexts.
- We can apply frameworks and taxonomies to analyze and classify culture.
- Public servants may find themselves managing difficult cultural challenges when working with different national cultures as well as collaborating with public private partnerships and/or agencies/networks.
- A managerial perspective on culture argues that it can be universal; created and shaped by strategy and leadership. A social scientist perspective on culture accepts a pluralist view made up of sub-cultures.
- Different cultures may suit different operating environments and will also be related to the function of the organization.
- Culture is a living thing, sometimes changing; it is a very slow process. Thus, the notion of managing culture is problematic.

KEY TERMS

- **Organizational culture** – a set of basic assumptions, expressed through values and resulting in accepted ways of working in an organization.
- **Ethical climate** – that part of organizational culture that relates to its ethical values.
- **Cultural relativism** – where ethical behaviour is determined by cultural context (i.e. 'when in Rome do as the Romans').
- **Ethical imperialism** – one version of values and ethics is imposed on another by those with the power and authority to do so.

INTRODUCTION

Some 40 years ago one of the authors of this book was a junior civil servant in the UK Home Office Prison Department. He was recruited by a white, middle-class, well-educated and primarily male selection panel that reflected the composition of the civil service as a whole at that time. The job consisted of working with architects, engineers and surveyors in constructing new prison extensions or refurbishing existing buildings. It involved providing administrative support, based mainly in a Whitehall office with the occasional on-site visit. He did, pretty much, what previous generations of civil servants had done in terms of following administrative procedures and learning on the job. The processes were standardized, and clear lines of authority were well established. He did not last longer than a year, finding the routine leaving little scope for deviations, distractions or digressions, all essential for a 19-year-old.

Of course, some fun was had by finding excuses, at any available opportunity, to talk with the architects, engineers and surveyors who seemed to follow different rules and were not bound by the hierarchy of the administrative class. They appeared to turn up late and leave early, wore brightly coloured bow ties and were more than happy to discuss the previous day's sports results. Strange people indeed! And yet, administrators (now called managers) working with professionals are common across the whole of the public sector, which begs the question, 'Is there one public sector culture or are there many?' Not only that but is there the possibility of conflict between the different cultures? Think of medical professionals who work alongside the administrative class. Professional loyalties and allegiances to colleagues and to patients may come into conflict with responsibilities to be financially prudent and to take into consideration the welfare of patients as a whole. This is part of what it means to manage in the public services.

The role of the civil servant touched upon above did not seem to change much long after your author left but by the mid-1990s the impact of public services reform, under the banner of New Public Management and discussed in more detail below and in Chapter 4, was evident. The civil service became more business-like in its activities and adopted values that were more usually associated with the private sector. Many have argued that the adoption of such values has had a detrimental effect on the public service ethos (see Frederickson 1993). We look at the changing values below.

We are interested in how culture, and values, might change, and how certain values might be sustained over time. We are also interested in the extent to which culture and values may differ between countries. Does the experience of our young civil servant above resonate with our understandings of the civil service elsewhere? Further, does the civil service culture differ from police culture, medical culture or social work culture?

WHAT IS CULTURE?

There are a number of models and frameworks to help us analyze culture (e.g. the classic iceberg model by French and Bell (1999); the onion model created by Hofstede (1991)). A widely used organizational culture framework is that of Schein (1990: 114). He described culture as a set of basic assumptions of a given group that may be invented, discovered or developed as the group seeks to align its external environment with its internal workings. Thus, a stable external environment may fit with a hierarchical organization that has clear lines of authority and operating procedures and clearly defined roles. Such internal processes and structure may not fit, however, with a rapidly changing, turbulent environment where quick decisions are required that are not part of the normal routines. Clearly different parts of the existing culture will determine how members of that organization respond to their environments. In Schein's model, culture exists on three levels:

Artefacts – which are difficult to measure and represent organizational attributes that can be observed, felt and heard as an individual enters a new culture. For example, executive car-parking spaces may be perceived to represent power and inequality. Likewise, for executive dining rooms or university senior common rooms. The arguments presented for such 'perks' may be rational and understandable but the symbolic statements that they make should not be underestimated.

Values – these are the espoused goals, ideals, norms, standards and moral principles that the organization proclaims, often measured through survey questionnaires.

Underlying assumptions – these are often difficult to explain to outsiders when members are asked about the culture of the organizations: 'This is the way we do things around here.' They are often taken for granted and remain unexplained, and unexplored. According to Schein, this is where organizational culture can be located. Complete Exercise 5.1.

> ## EXERCISE 5.1 APPLYING CULTURAL ANALYSIS
>
> Think of a public service organization that you either work in or have experienced and apply Schein's typology by providing examples of artefacts, values and underlying assumptions that are implicit of the culture.

Culture can be transmitted over time, and across space, through different mechanisms, and these will consist of both deliberate and informal processes. The deliberate mechanisms will operate through, for example, the recruitment processes, the promotion processes, training, organizational codes of conduct and values statements. The informal processes will work through the myths and stories that are handed down from one generation of staff to the next, through the group norms and the practices that by-pass the formal ways of working. Thus, introducing service-level agreements between departments in the same local authority or municipality may undermine the informal arrangements of helping out a colleague elsewhere on the understanding that at some future time, the favour will be returned. Which way of working is more efficient or effective?

Culture change is difficult: it involves changing attitudes, beliefs and values; all the things that are important to individuals and define them as individuals. Thus we are saying that organizational culture consists of, and helps shape, individual values. Culture is not something that an organization has, but is a living thing – sometimes changing; it is a very slow process, e.g. the British civil service. Thus, the notion of managing culture is problematic. This is explored in Exercise 5.2.

> ## EXERCISE 5.2 MANAGING CULTURE
>
> One of the authors worked in a university department where the students did not have access to the lecturers. The offices of the lecturers were behind locked doors and the students had to book an appointment with their lecturer through the reception desk. At the appointed time the lecturer would emerge from behind the locked doors and meet their students in an open area where similar meetings were taking place between other lecturers and their students. Despite repeated attempts to change this practice by a new head of department the lecturing staff refused to budge. It was the one discussion item that was guaranteed to raise emotions at departmental meetings.
>
> ■ Question: What do you think of this practice and what reasons can be given for or against support of it?

ORGANIZATIONAL CULTURE: THE DEBATE

One view of culture is that it can be integrated and managed to achieve an organization-wide consensus; a second view sees culture as differentiated, consisting of sub-cultures that might be defined along occupational roles (Parker and Bradley 2000). These contrasting viewpoints or two perspectives concerning culture can be categorized as a managerial and social scientist perspective (Huczynski and Buchanan 2007). The managerial perspective argues there is a relationship between a strong culture and organizational performance and people can be socialized, bringing about 'stronger organizational commitment, higher morale, more efficient performance, and generally higher productivity' (Furnham and Gunter 1993: 232). Therefore, it takes a normative and prescriptive stance. Management strategy is created to guide behaviour and the processes within the organization, and recommends what these should be with the aim of achieving a unitary perspective of consistencies and consensus throughout the organization. This managerial view argues that

> every organization has a culture comprising objective reality of artefacts, values and meanings that academics can quantify and measure. . . . it is given to its members when they join, and they do not participate in its formation.
> (Huczynski and Buchanan 2007: 634)

In contrast, the social science view draws on culture to explain differences between organizations, and argues that it is a subjective reality; it has rites, rituals and meanings, is symbolic and takes a social constructivist perspective. As such, it is not objective and cannot be easily quantified or measured. Moreover, it recognizes sub-cultures within organizations and therefore takes a pluralistic perspective.

Another way of analyzing culture commonly found in the literature is using taxonomies, and we find differences between bureaucratic, market and clan cultures (Ouchi 1981). Bureaucratic cultures are typically found in large organizations, operating in a stable environment, characterized by hierarchical lines of accountability and responsibility and are process-focused. Market cultures are driven by the external competitive environment, are typically flexible and responsive to an unstable environment, with shorter reporting lines, and are results-focused. Clan cultures have a long history and a stable membership such that knowledge and values are passed on from one generation to the next. There is frequent interaction amongst members, goal congruence over the longer term and it works well in conditions of ambiguity and complexity.

Many organizations exhibit all three types of culture, but for the purpose of simplicity, Table 5.1 captures the main features of these different types of cultures.

We are not saying that one culture is, in some sense, better than another; rather different cultures may suit different operating environments. Culture will also be

Table 5.1 *Organizational features and culture*

	Bureaucracy	Market	Clan
Authority system	Position-centred, rank hierarchical	Person-centred, expertise	Person-centred, loyalty, participative
Task focus	Repetition, standardization, specialization	Innovation	Knowledge-centred
Orientation	Rules-oriented	Results-oriented, performance-driven	Relationship-orientated
Reward system	Status and rank	Value-added and meeting targets	Peer recognition
Information flows	Formal structures	Market information	Open information
Style	Territorial, centralized	Competition	Cohesion and collegiality
Decision-making	Hierarchy and rules	Negotiation and bargaining	Obligations to colleagues
Competency	Skills-based professional	Relational, sceptical of professional judgement	Professional judgement
Dysfunctions	Rule-bending or hiding behind rules	Customer rather than citizen-focused	'Jobs for the boys'

related to the function of the organization. Sometimes this can be problematic. Our young civil servant was working in a government department whose purpose was two-fold; first, to punish offenders for their crimes, and second, to rehabilitate offenders so that they return to society at the end of their sentences as responsible citizens. Clearly, these may be in conflict and it is not unusual to find diverse missions within the same public service organization. Table 5.2 illustrates the different types of public service organizations.

ETHICAL CLIMATE

The ethical climate of an organization is generally considered to be that part of culture that relates to its ethical values. It has been defined as

> the shared set of understandings about what is correct behaviour and how ethical issues will be handled. This climate sets the tone for decision making at all levels and in all circumstances.

> (Sims 1992: 510)

Table 5.2 *Organizational type*

Type of organization	Who does it affect?	What is its prime motivation?	Features	Cultural type
Regulatory, e.g. licensing, taxation	Individuals; Organizations	Rules-based	Some discretion	Predominantly bureaucratic
Welfare services (individual), e.g. social security	Individuals	Caring and benevolence	Professional judgement	Clan
Welfare services (collective), e.g. environmental protection	Society	Public interest	Policy-making	Bureaucracy
Security, e.g. policing	Individuals; Organizations; Society	Justice, law and order; Public interest	Hierarchy with operational independence	Bureaucracy and clan
Support services, e.g. finance	Organization as a whole	Organization interests	Focus on centralized decision-making	Bureaucracy
Regional development	Society	Public interest	Local focus	Bureaucracy; Market
Trading agency	Individuals	Generating a surplus	Entrepreneurial	Market

According to this definition it is concerned with some notion of, ethically, the right behaviour, and will be reflected in the organization's policies, practices and the decisions that are made. It will be influenced by all of those factors, both internal and external that shape how an organization operates. Externally these will be laws and professional codes; internally they will include personal self-interest/morality, organizational goals, operating practices, individual friendships, team interests, rules and standard procedures, leadership, structure, institutional policies, incentive systems, decision-making processes, informal norms. In the relationship between the individual and the organization we might ask: Does the climate encourage individuals to look out for their self-interests? Does it support professional norms or support autonomous personal norms and beliefs? Is there an attitude of protecting the organization at all costs? How does the organization treat its internal and external stakeholders? We could also consider what an unethical climate might look like, and its features might include: condoning illegal or unethical acts; demoralized staff; lack of concern and support for colleagues, clients or citizens; self-interest exercised by individuals or by cliques; no positive leadership example; a perverse reward system based on narrow performance indicators such as number of complaints and/or time taken to deal with complaints; or 'buck-passing'.

The outcomes of the ethical climate will impact organizational commitment, job satisfaction, staff stress and psychological well-being, staff turnover, efficiency and effectiveness. Cullen, Victor and Stephens (2001) argue that the factors that determine ethical climate are the environment in which the organization functions, the form of the organization (e.g. centralized or divisionalized) and the organization's history.

Research by the Ethics Resource Center[1] (2010) found that ethical culture is experienced differently by different kinds of employees. It is perceived to be stronger within a company by managers and senior leaders, non-unionized workers, older workers, and most-tenured employees. The research also found that the actions and perceptions of top managers drive the ethical culture of the company and have a significant impact on outcomes, although this also depends on the size of the organization. For example, the more layers within the organization the less direct influence top management may have because of in-between levels of managers. A third finding was that co-worker culture (that is, the influencing norms and employees' interactions with co-workers) is particularly powerful for decreasing observations of financial misconduct, but top management culture is associated with the greater increase in reporting it. The research was based upon private sector companies and found that when it comes to the strength of ethical culture some companies are at an innate disadvantage. Thus, those companies most likely to have a strong ethical culture are those with non-unionized workers, fewer than 500 employees, privately held, and have employee-owners. In contrast those companies most likely to have a weak or weak-leaning ethical culture are highly unionized, with 500+ employees, are publicly traded and those where employees do not hold stock. Now look at Exercise 5.3.

EXERCISE 5.3 DIMENSIONS OF ETHICAL CLIMATE

Jones and James (1979) identify six dimensions to ethical climate:

(i)   Leadership facilitation and support
(ii) Workgroup co-operation, friendliness and warmth
(iii) Conflict and ambiguity
(iv) Professional and organization *esprit*
(v)   Job challenge, importance and variety
(vi) Mutual trust

To what extent are these dimensions of 'good management' rather than ethical management?

Table 5.3 *Ethical climate types*

Ethical criterion	Locus of analysis		
	Individual	Local	Cosmopolitan
Egoism	Self-interest	Company profit	Efficiency
Benevolence	Friendship	Team interest	Social responsibility
Principle	Personal morality	Company rules and procedures	Laws and professional codes

Source: Victor and Cullen (1988: 104)

The ethical climate of an organization has been subject to measurement and the best-known tool is the Ethical Climate Questionnaire developed by Cullen, Victor and Bronson (1993). It is well established and uses a number of constructs developed from Kohlberg's work on ethical decision-making and moral reasoning that we discussed in Chapter 2. The constructs are egoism, based on self-interested behaviour; benevolence in caring for others and reflecting utilitarianism; and principles, based on acting according to principles irrespective of consequences and reflecting a deontological approach to moral reasoning. The locus of analysis is at three levels and reflects three different sources of moral influence. First, the individual's own beliefs; second, the local organization's standards and policies; and third, bodies external to the organization, expressed as cosmopolitan influences. These can be expressed in a tabular form (see Table 5.3).

All nine ethical climate types do occur but Victor and Cullen (1988) concluded that most likely to be found were: law and code, based on some external mandate; caring, based upon the welfare of others; instrumentalism, based upon self-interest or the interests of the organization; independence, acting on personal moral beliefs; and rules, based on company procedures.

Research carried out by the New South Wales Independent Commission Against Corruption (ICAC) found that an organization has the potential to make an ethical person act unethically. Based upon surveys, the research asked which features are most strongly associated with perceptions of the workplace being honest. The findings include:

— Behaviour of leaders; act honestly, practice what they preach, encourage new ideas, treat staff fairly and equally, give them scope to make decisions.
— Punishment of wrongdoing; appropriate action taken.
— Existence of organizational values, rule and rewards; true to values, fostering the development of staff, leading to greater job satisfaction, a greater willingness to stay in the job, feeling safe and willing to express their opinions, feeling safe to report wrongdoing, better relationships with supervisors and colleagues.

The ICAC research argued for 'open', rather than 'closed' leadership expressed through encouraging staff participation, relinquishing of control, inviting and accepting criticism, encouraging divergent ideas, acting as advisers or facilitators, establishing a climate where staff can express their own views.

COMPARING CULTURES BETWEEN COUNTRIES

Notwithstanding our discussion of ethical relativism in Chapter 2, a key issue is the extent to which ethical issues are universal in their scope and scale. Does the public official in South Africa face the same ethical issues as those in Lithuania or Mexico; do they, indeed, have the same understanding of ethics? If not, can we make any meaningful cross-country comparisons in the field of ethics or can we learn from each other no matter how tenuous the similarities? We know an increasing amount about the different ethical or integrity frameworks that exist in different countries around the world, helped by participation in a number of international conferences and workshops that have been devoted to such matters as the Ethics and Integrity of Governance study group at the European Group of Public Administration annual conference.[2]

An impressive number of country studies have introduced us to a wide range of policy instruments used to, for example, combat corruption or to uphold standards of conduct through codification. The extent to which we have learnt from each other, however, or the extent to which a universal theory of, say, ethical regulation, has been developed, is a moot point. Moreover, cultural relativism takes the view that behaviour is determined by its cultural context and as such, there is no definitive right or wrong way to behave. Hence, no culture's ethics can claim superiority as the norms, values and practices within the cultural context determine what is right or wrong. This view can be contrasted with ethical universality that claims that we can determine what is right or wrong as there are certain absolute truths that apply everywhere and universal values transcend cultures. The problem with this latter approach is that it is a short step to ethical imperialism which seeks to judge others by our own standards and to impose those standards on others.

Much of the research has been on single-country studies or has been descriptive, taking the form of 'this is what country x or country y does to curb corruption or enhance trust in government'. We do not know enough on the extent to which countries are converging in their approach to ethics. There are also international barometers of ethics such as those developed by Transparency International's integrity index,[3] based upon perceptual surveys, but such surveys tend to be uninformative as an explanation of why certain countries are in certain positions in the league tables, or why they move up and down the league tables. Further research may illuminate the importance of the role that ethical leadership has to play in these movements and other issues such as economic factors that may influence position.

Convergence can be described as the tendency for countries to grow more alike, to develop similarities in structure, processes and performance (Bennett 1991). It may be both temporal and spatial and is a dynamic process. It means moving from different positions to a common point and such a common point may be one that is normative and considered desirable by international agencies such as the World Bank. One of your authors was involved in a project to develop an ethical framework in Lithuania, funded by the EU, as a condition of entry into the EU. One example of a comparative approach has been used to explore the extent to which changes in public services reform under the rubric of NPM have become universalized. This resonates with global attempts at ethics reforms. Thus, the claims to universality are said to depend upon a number of conditions. First, the adoption of the same set of doctrines as the means to solve the problems of traditional public administration. Second, that reforms are apolitical and are supported by politicians of all hues. Third, that problems in one country are similar, and linked to, problems in other countries. Fourth, that there is a new global paradigm replacing commonly held assumptions bringing in a new agenda, values and policies. All of these can be applied to ethics regimes and all are contested.

For many scholars, the main line of enquiry appears to be to identify key aspects of NPM as discussed in the literature, and then look for their existence in particular countries. These aspects are said to include the use of markets and deregulation (Steane 2008); contracting and citizen charters (McCourt 2008); and the use of agencies to enhance managerial freedoms (Verschuere and Barbieri 2009). There appears to be general agreement that reforms have been more readily accepted in some countries, including Australia, New Zealand, the US, Canada and the UK (e.g. Pollitt and Bouckaert 2004). Nevertheless, even amongst this group, it is argued, there are differences. Lynn (2006), for example, argues that NPM in the US focused on managerial discretion, quality and entrepreneurship and far less on market-mimicking reforms that had long been popular anyway.

In other countries individual elements have taken hold, depending upon a number of factors. These include the political, social and legal context of the State that determines the kind of reforms that are adopted. Thus, Wenzel (2007), for example, argues that in many countries it is the centralization and personalization of political power that determines whether reform will take place and shapes that reform. Schedler and Proeller (2002) distinguish between unitary, centralist and federalist States and Verschuere and Barbieri (2009), in their research on agencies, argue that it is country-specific factors that determine reform processes. Some authors make use of Hofstede's typology of cultural differences to explore country differences (Flynn 2002; Pollitt and Bouckaert 2004; Verschuere and Barbieri 2009) and we look at this later in this chapter.

A second set of reasons refers to the imposition of reforms by international agencies on reluctant recipients that cause problems, and scholars working in the development field have long lamented the impact of organizations such as the

World Bank, OECD (PUMA) and IMF. They have pushed an international vocabulary with terms such as 'agentification', 'contractualization', 'performance measurement' and 'privatization' (Pollitt and Bouckaert 2004). The scope of reform, the role of aid donors and the leadership of change are examined by Polidano (2001). He argues that 'Grand Design' can often drive out local reforms. In his view the World Bank comes up with a solution in search of a problem – foisting the solution on to a client government is problematic. In a similar fashion, Batley (1999) argues that the reform agenda is too easily captured by those with a stake in applying reform (donors, consultants, etc.). This approach can provide a bedrock for ethical imperialism.

Polidano (1999) argues that, in the context of the developing world, NPM is only one of a number of currents of reform and suggests that its universal character has long been contested. He suggests a number of questions that need to be addressed and we paraphrase and develop these questions to consider the ethical dimension to reforms.

– Are developing countries committing themselves to ethical reforms?
– Are reforms part of the worldwide quest for efficiency and effectiveness or are they being undertaken for different reasons?
– Are they being implemented or are we being misled by the rhetoric? Lynn (2006) argues that NPM uses similarities in rhetoric to exaggerate similarities in practice.
– Are there other reforms that are being undertaken that might undermine ethical reforms? For example, does the move to market economies provide more opportunities for corruption and fraud?
– Are the problems that ethical reform is said to address the same in all countries? For example, in some countries personnel problems are the issue when recruitment and promotion reflect nepotism or seniority rather than competence. In others, low pay of public officials will be a problem.

Pollitt (2002) focuses on the notion of convergence and identifies four stages of convergence. These are, first, *discursive convergence*, such that more and more people are using the same concepts. Second, *decisional convergence*, where different authorities adopt similar organizational forms or techniques. Third, *practice convergence*, insofar as organizations begin to work in similar ways. Fourth, *results convergence*, where the outputs and outcomes of public service organizations begin to look similar. Pollitt argues that while there may be convergence in discursive and decisional convergence, there is less evidence of convergence in terms of practice or results.

Now let us turn to a more specific discussion of convergence and differences in culture and what this might mean for ethics. Geert Hofstede carried out a study of 117,000 IBM employees across 72 national subsidiaries in 66 countries. Table 5.4 describes the different dimensions used in this research and provides some indication

Table 5.4 Dimensions and features of culture

Dimension	Description	Features (high)	Examples (high)	Features (low)	Examples (low)	Ethical implications
Power distance	The extent to which the less powerful members of institutions and organizations accept that power is distributed unevenly	Hierarchical; autocratic decision-making style; inequalities expected and accepted	Malaysia, China, India, Mexico	Consultative relationship, mutuality, decentralization	Australia, US, Norway, Netherlands	Individuals in high power distance cultures will be influenced by superiors rather than peers and will follow formal codes rather than informal norms
Uncertainty avoidance	How comfortable people feel towards ambiguity; made nervous by unclear or unpredictable situations	Avoid ambiguity; importance of rules, reduction of conflict	Greece, Belgium, Japan	Take risks for high rewards, comfortable with ambiguity, open-ended learning, tolerant	Jamaica, Denmark, UK, Malaysia, India	Individuals in high uncertainty avoidance cultures are more likely to follow rules and less likely to perceive ethical problems
Masculinity and femininity	Expected gender roles of men as assertive and ambitious and expect women to serve	Masculine cultures value independence, aggressiveness, dominance and physical strength, assertive, tough, competitive	Japan, Italy, Ireland, Arab world, Germany, UK	Feminine cultures value interdependence, compassion, empathy, focus on relationship	Thailand, Costa Rica, Sweden, Chile, Portugal, Netherlands	Individuals in cultures that are high in masculinity are less likely to perceive ethical problems and less influenced by formal codes
Individualism and collectivism	Extent to which individual behaviours are influenced by others	Individual interest prevail over those of the group, more regard for assertiveness, individual freedom and self-actualization	US, Australia, France, Sweden, Canada, UK	Emphasis on family, clan, the group, harmony and consensus	Ecuador, Panama, Indonesia, South Korea	Individuals in Individualist societies are more likely to pursue self-interest and be less constrained by rules and norms

of the key features of those countries that are either high or low on the dimension. Table 5.4 also provides some examples of countries identified in each category. The list is not exhaustive and the full research can be found in Hofstede (1980, 1991).

Commentary

Despite its influence, the work of Hofstede has been criticized. Methodologically, although the overall numbers that responded to the survey were large, it was only in six countries that there were more than 1,000 respondents and in 15 countries there were less than 200 respondents. All the respondents were employed by one company, IBM, and it is a moot point whether culture was uniform or made up of many sub-cultures. The research also assumes bipolarity (i.e. either masculinity or femininity), whereas it is possible that seemingly opposite features can co-exist in the same culture. Although Hofstede's approach allows us to analyze cross-cultural values, his seminal research has been updated and extended by the Global Leadership and Organizational Effectiveness (GLOBE) research programme (Javidon and House 2001). This is a longitudinal study in 62 countries of 825 organizations. GLOBE's framework goes beyond the dimensions of Hofstede's work to include assertiveness, future orientation, performance orientation and humane orientation.

In a slightly less ambitious research project, De Vries (2002) looked at honesty in local government in 17 countries, primarily European-based with the exception of Japan and Korea. The research included almost 10,000 respondents. We present some of the findings in Table 5.5.

One of the key findings of the research was that the association between abstract principles and the translation into rules for everyday practice is, at best, partial. The research indicated that ethics is less an individual trait than a social trait determined by what is customary within the organization. Despite the issues associated with comparative cultures and comparative ethics, a brief search of the values statements from public service agencies from around the world reveals similarities. See Box 5.1 for examples, and then look at Exercise 5.4 and answer the following questions.

Questions

■ What has prevented some of Chicago's public sector leaders from adopting an ethical culture?
■ What could be done to bring about a recognizable ethical culture in this situation?

Table 5.5 *Honesty in local government*

Country	Honesty and truthfulness must never be compromised at any cost	Leaders should present the truth no matter what the consequences	Local leaders should always publicly and truthfully speak the facts about their failures in performing public affairs	To avoid misunderstanding a leader should not disclose certain facts	To achieve community goals it is permissible for leaders to present facts in a one-sided way
Korea	99.3		97.8	24.9	
Hungary	92.8	60.4	87.0	67.5	10.5
Japan	90.7	96.2	90.5	35.3	19.3
Slovenia	92.0	71.5	84.4	72.6	2.9
The Netherlands	93.8	82.7	81.1	22.5	14.0
Sweden	96.6	97.0	80.5	11.6	11.3
Turkey	98.6	91.1	94.6	44.9	54.6

Responses represent percentages that agree/strongly agree

BOX 5.1   VALUE STATEMENTS

The Victoria Department of Justice in Australia is committed to:

1. Serving the community
2. Working together
3. Acting with integrity

   And will:

   - Accept accountability for our actions
   - Be honest, fair and reliable
   - Approach our work with enthusiasm and commitment
   - Apply sound judgement and common sense
   - Embrace personal and professional development

4. Respecting other people

   And will:

   - Treat all people with respect
   - Seek different perspectives and approaches
   - Value work/life balance
   - Give and receive feedback constructively
   - Show consideration for each other's ideas and contributions

5. Making it happen.

The **New York City Law Department** is committed to public service through values and these are dedication, diversity, environment, excellence, integrity, professional development, respecting supportive work and team work.

The **Johannesburg Revenue and Customer Relations Management Department** is committed to SPIRIT:

Service: to meet expectations by consistently contributing to the satisfaction and well-being of customers, staff and colleagues in a passionate, courteous and knowledgeable manner

Professionalism: to take pride in what we do by providing the highest level of service to everyone we encounter

Integrity: to consistently act honourably and above reproach and to ensure that we keep the promises that we make

Respect: to maintain a high regard for our staff, colleagues and customers in our daily engagements

Integration: to maintain one voice to stakeholders through a shared understanding of vision, values and goals, to ensure the smooth co-ordination of activities across functions and channels

Team work: to actively engage the spirit of co-operation to ensure we remain a team that always works through collective leadership and effective communication.

EXERCISE 5.4   A CULTURE OF CORRUPTION

Katie Connolly from *BBC News* (2010) wrote, 'Political corruption and Chicago go together like fashion and Milan or surfers and Sydney: the association is deep, and it has shaped the city. Most Illinois historians date the corruption back to 1869, when three county commissioners were convicted of fraudulently awarding a contract to paint City Hall with expensive long lasting paint. The contractor instead used whitewash, and split the handsome price difference with the three commissioners. And then it rained. Suddenly the gleaming white City Hall didn't look so spiffy.'

Since 1970, there have been more than 1,500 convictions on public corruption charges in Illinois courts. 'Everyone from Chicago aldermen and building inspectors to State governors has been involved,' stated Dick Simpson, a former Chicago alderman.

'The State was founded on favours' (Cindy Canary, director for Illinois Campaign for Political Reform).

The first wave of immigrants helped set up government and infrastructure, and soon encouraged their countyfolk to join them. They aided newcomers, providing jobs and securing housing. As elections unfolded in the State, the power of these ethnic voting blocks became evident. Members of the Irish community voted for Irish candidates and were rewarded with jobs in the police force. The Italian community voted for Italian candidates, who rewarded their own with jobs setting up Chicago's transit system, and so on. 'The culture of corruption from machine politics is helped by essentially one-party rule, that sets in motion a problem where bribes and the like are more likely to flourish because the public officials can't tell the difference between what might be legal in campaigns and what is illegal when they seek money for public acts,' Mr Simpson says.

Rod Blagojevich was elected governor of Illinois in 2002 and served until 2009, when the State legislature threw him out of his office following his arrest in December 2008. In FBI wire taps, Blagojevich was heard describing the Senate appointment as a 'golden' opportunity. He was subsequently convicted of trying to extort campaign donations from business executives, and of soliciting bribes from racing officials. Prosecutors said, 'Blagojevich engaged in extensive criminal conduct . . . provided no co-operation, perjured himself for seven days on the witness stand, and has accepted no responsibility for his criminal conduct.'

His Republican predecessor as governor was also jailed for corruption. Pleading for leniency before sentencing, Blagojevich told the judge he 'never set out to break the law' and that what he thought he had been doing was 'permissible'.

Source: adapted from Connolly (2010) and BBC (2011)

COMPARING CULTURES BETWEEN SECTORS

One of the oft-quoted but under-researched contentions is that public service reforms, like some of those we discussed above under the rubric of New Public Management, have a detrimental effect on public service values. We follow van der Wal, De Graaf and Lasthuizen (2008: 468) in defining values as 'important qualities and standards that have a weight in the choice of action'. Clearly such values may be ethical or they may not. For example, efficiency is a key instrumental value of organizations, but is it an ethical value? The consequences of being inefficient in the public services may have ethical consequences insofar as wasted resources could have been used to provide welfare for a greater number of people, but the concept of efficiency itself is not necessarily ethical. To criticize an individual for being inefficient carries a different weight than criticizing an individual for being dishonest. Thus we might want to distinguish between ethical values such as integrity and honesty, democratic values such as the rule of law and impartiality, organizational values such as efficiency and effectiveness, and professional values such as caring and expertise.

Moreover, van der Wal *et al.* (2008) identified a set of 20 organizational values and we reproduce these in Box 5.2.

BOX 5.2   MIXED SET OF PUBLIC, PRIVATE AND COMMON CORE ORGANIZATIONAL VALUES

Organizational value set

Accountability: act willingly to justify and explain actions to the relevant stakeholders

Collegiality: act loyally and show solidarity towards colleagues

Dedication: act with diligence, enthusiasm and perseverance

Effectiveness: act to achieve the desired results

Efficiency: act to achieve results with minimal means

Expertise: act with competence, skill and knowledge

Honesty: act truthfully and comply with promises

Impartiality: act without prejudice or bias towards specific group interests

Incorruptibility: act without prejudice and bias towards private interests

Innovativeness: act with initiative and creativity (to invent or introduce new policies or products)

Lawfulness: act in accordance with existing laws and rules

Obedience: act in compliance with the instructions and policies (of superiors and the organization)

Profitability: act to achieve gain (financial or other)

Reliability: act in a trustworthy and consistent way towards relevant stakeholders

Responsiveness: act in accordance with the preferences of citizens and customers

Self-fulfilment: act to stimulate the (professional) development and well-being of employees

Serviceability: act helpfully and offer quality and service towards citizens and customers

Social justice: act out of commitment to a just society

Sustainability: act out of commitment to nature and the environment

Transparency: act openly, visibly and controllably

Source: Van der Wal et al. (2008: 470)

Using this set of values the authors then compared and contrasted public and private sector values, and we represent some of their findings in Table 5.6. In bold are those values that are common to both sectors.

Is there anything that is surprising in their findings?

Table 5.6 *Public and private sector values*

Public sector (most important)	Private sector (most important)	Public sector (least important)	Private sector (least important)
Accountability	Profitability	Profitability	Self-fulfilment
Lawfulness	**Accountability**	Self-fulfilment	Social justice
Incorruptibility	**Reliability**	Social justice	Obedience
Expertise	**Effectiveness**	Obedience	Impartiality
Reliability	**Expertise**	Sustainability	Sustainability
Effectiveness	**Efficiency**	Responsiveness	Responsiveness
Impartiality	Honesty	Innovativeness	Serviceability
Efficiency	Innovativeness	Honesty	Collegiality

Commentary

Clearly not all values are necessarily ethical in character; yet 'honesty' as one of the least important for public sector employees is surprising. Both public sector and private sector organizations share a number of organizational values but the research does not indicate that traditional public service values of accountability, lawfulness, incorruptibility or impartiality have been eroded by 20 years of public service reform. Similarly, despite the rhetoric of NPM responsiveness it is not considered to be a key public service value. At the same time, responsiveness and serviceability are low down on the list of private sector values; so much for the much-trumpeted notion that the customer is always king or queen. Similarly, there is little room for team work/collegiality as part of the private sector values and we might wonder what chance public/private partnerships might have in the absence of such values.

CHANGING CULTURE

Let us start with a general observation regarding change:

It must be considered that there is nothing more difficult to carry out, nor more doubtful to success, than to initiate a new order of things. For the reformer has enemies in all those who profit by the old order, and only lukewarm defenders in all those who profit by the new order, this lukewarmness arising partly from fear of their adversaries, who have the laws in their favour; and partly from the incredulity of mankind, who do not truly believe in anything new until they have actual experience of it.

(Machiavelli 2005 [1516]: 24)

Machiavelli would recommend, in modern language, a change strategy which might include incentive systems, training programmes, restructuring, appointing new staff and so on. We have discussed the resilience of traditional values and there are limits to the capacity to initiate and implement change. We must also consider what might be lost in such a process. Consider the following description of a civil service culture:

[I]n every Department [there is] a store of knowledge and experience in the subjects handled, something which eventually takes shape as a practical philosophy, or may merit the title of a departmental philosophy . . . in most cases the departmental philosophy is nothing more startling than the slow accretion and accumulation of experience over the years.

(Bridges 1950: 16)

Such a 'slow accretion and accumulation', though, may lead to ossification of the existing culture such that the organization fails to keep up with a rapidly changing environment, or that existing unethical practices become embedded within the fabric of the organization and are condoned. Unethical behaviour may be rewarded – remember Enron? And, there may be a lack of sanctions for such behaviour.

There are a number of prescriptions for developing an ethical culture and these will include:

- finding ethical 'champions' at the top of the organization or gaining support of those at senior levels
- setting values and goals that are realistic and not utopian
- communicating open and transparently
- allowing individuals to be consulted when developing values statements and codes of conduct
- treating all employees as trusted and valuable individuals with opportunities to reach their full potential
- encouraging diversity and dissent and different viewpoints
- introducing appropriate practices to develop an ethical culture and support employees, such as whistle-blowing procedures
- introducing ethics training for all staff
- recognize that ethics is full of grey areas

— integrating ethical decision-making into the performance-appraisal process. Most organizations are quick to condemn unethical behaviour but ethical behaviour is rarely rewarded.

CONCLUSIONS

Cultures are dynamic and we should anticipate the existence of sub-cultures within organizations. It may be neither desirable nor feasible to build a strong and unified sense of values. Without doubt culture is an elusive concept and the extent to which it can be managed will remain contested. We know that we need to understand it if we are to make sense of how the complex organizations that deliver public services work. From the ethical point of view, individual values, organizational values and wider social values will come together in the mix. It is evident, increasingly, that working in such organizations requires a sensitivity to, and empathy with, diverse groups of individuals in other organizations and in other geographical spaces. When we factor in the need to understand how cultures develop over time it becomes clear that to capture the ethical climate of an organization through a snapshot is problematic. At the very least scholars will need to carry out longitudinal studies and to employ comparative methodology to begin to make sense of changes across time and space.

NOTES

1   http://www.ethics.org/
2   http://www.law.kuleuven.be/linc/integriteit/egpa/
3   http://www.transparency.org/whatwedo/tools/

REFERENCES

Batley, R. (1999) 'The New Public Management in Developing Countries: Implications for Policy and Organizational Reform', *Journal of International Development* 11 (5): 761–5.

BBC (2011) 'Rod Blagojevich Sentenced to 14 Years in Prison', 7 December. Available at: www.bbc.co.uk/news/world-15602816 (accessed 26 July 2012).

Bennett, C.J. (1991) 'What is Policy Convergence and What Causes It?' *British Journal of Political Science* 21 (2): 215–33.

Bridges, E. Sir (1950) *Portrait of a Profession*. Cambridge: Cambridge University Press.

Cullen, J.B., Victor, B. and Bronson, J.W. (1993) 'The Ethical Climate Questionnaire: An Assessment of Its Development and Validity', *Psychological Reports* 73 (2): 667–74.

Cullen, J.B., Victor, B. and Stephens, C. (2001) 'An Ethical Weather Report: Assessing the Organization's Ethical Climate', *Organizational Dynamics* 18: 50–62.

Connolly, K. (2010) 'Why is Illinois So Often Corrupt?' BBC, 18 August. Available at: www.bbc.co.uk/news/world-us-canada-11016677 (accessed 26 July 2012).

De Vries, M.S. (2002) 'Can You Afford Honesty? A Comparative Analysis of Ethos and Ethics in Local Government', *Administration and Society* 34 (3): 309–34.

Ethics Resource Center (2010) *The Importance of Ethical Culture: Increasing Trust and Driving Down Risks*. 2009 National Business Ethics Survey. Arlington, VA: Ethics Resource Center.

Flynn, N. (2002) 'Explaining the New Public Management: The Importance of Context' in McLaughlin, K., Osborne, S.P. and Ferlie, E. (eds) *New Public Management: Current Trends and Future Prospects*. London and New York: Routledge, pp. 57–76.

Frederickson, H.G. (1993) 'Ethics and Public Administration: Some Assertions' in Frederickson, H.G. (ed.) *Ethics and Public Administration*. New York: M.E. Sharpe, pp. 243–62.

French, W.L. and Bell, C.W. (1999) *Organization Development: Behavioural Science Interventions for Organizational Improvement*. 6th edition. New Delhi: PHI Learning.

Furnham, A. and Gunter, B. (1993) 'Corporate Culture: Definition, Diagnosis and Change' in Cooper, C.L. and Robertson, I.T. (eds) *International Review of Organizational Psychology* 8: 233–61.

Hofstede, G. (1980) *Culture's Consequences: International Differences in Work-related Values*. Beverley Hills, CA: Sage.

Hofstede, G. (1991) *Culture and Organizations*. Beverly Hills, CA: Sage.

Huczynski, A.A. and Buchanan, D.A. (2007) *Organizational Behavior*. 6th edition. New Jersey: Prentice Hall.

Javidon, M. and House, R.J. (2001) 'Cultural Acumen from the Global Manager: Lessons from the Project GLOBE', *Organizational Dynamics* 29 (4): 289–3.

Jones, A. and James, L. (1979) 'Psychological Climate: Dimensions and Relationships of Individual and Aggregated Work Environment Perceptions', *Organizational Behavior and Human Performance* 23 (2): 201–50.

Lynn, L.E. Jr. (2006) *Public Management: Old and New*. New York: Routledge.

Machiavelli, N. (2005) *The Prince*, ed. W.J. Connell. 1st Edition. New York: Bedford/ St. Martin's.

McCourt, W. (2008) 'Public Management in Developing Countries: From Downsizing to Governance', *Public Management Review* 10 (4): 467–79.

Ouchi, W. (1981) *Theory Z*. Reading, MA: Addison-Wesley.

Parker, R. and Bradley, L. (2000) 'Organizational Culture in the Public Sector: Evidence from Six Organizations', *The International Journal of Public Sector Management* 13 (2): 125–41.

Polidano, C. (1999) 'The New Public Management in Developing Countries', Public Policy and Management Working Paper no 13. Institute for Development Policy and Management, University of Manchester.

Polidano, C. (2001) 'Why Civil Service Reforms Fail', *Public Management Review* 3 (3): 345–61.

Polidano, C. and Hume, D. (2001) 'Editorial: Towards a Post-new Public Management Agenda', *Public Management Review* 3 (3): 297–303.

Pollitt, C. (2002) 'Clarifying Convergence: Striking Similarities and Durable Differences in Public Management Reform', *Public Management Review* 3 (4): 471–92.

Pollitt, C. and Bouckaert, G. (2004) *Public Management Reform: A Comparative Analysis*. 2nd edition. Oxford: Oxford University Press.

Schedler, K. and Proeller, I. (2002) 'The New Public Management: A Perspective from Mainland Europe' in McLaughlin, K., Osborne, S.P. and Ferlie, E. (eds) *New Public Management: Current Trends and Future Prospects*. London and New York: Routledge, pp. 163–80.

Schein, E.H. (1990) 'Organizational Culture', *American Psychologist* 45 (2): 109–19.

Sims, R.R. (1992) 'The Challenge of Ethical Behaviour in Organizations', *Journal of Business Ethics* 11 (7): 505–13.

Steane, P. (2008) 'Public Management Reforms in Australia and New Zealand: A Pot-pourri Overview of the Past Decade', *Public Management Review* 10 (4): 453–65.

van der Wal, Z., De Graaf, G. and Lasthuizen, K. (2008) 'What's Valued Most? Similarities and Differences Between the Organizational Values of the Public and Private Sector', *Public Administration* 86 (2): 465–82.

Verschuere, B. and Barbieri, D. (2009) 'Investigating the "NPM-ness" of Agencies in Italy and Flanders: The Effect of Place, Age and Task', *Public Management Review* 11 (3): 345–73.

Victor, B. and Cullen, J.B. (1988) 'The Organizational Bases of Ethical Work Climates', *Administrative Science Quarterly* 33 (1): 101–25.

Wenzel, P. (2007) 'Public-sector Transformation in South Africa: Getting the Basics Right', *Progress in Development Studies* 7 (1): 47–64.

Wittner, D. and Coursey, D. (1996) 'Ethical Work Climates: Comparing Top Managers in Public and Private Organizations', *Journal of Public Administration Research and Theory* 6 (4): 559–72.

Chapter 6

Compliance approaches
How can we enforce ethical standards and behaviour?

LEARNING OBJECTIVES

By the end of this chapter you should:

■ be able to describe the nature of ethical guidance, including self-regulation, codes of conduct and regulatory agencies

■ be able to analyze what form of regulation is appropriate and under what circumstances

■ begin to develop a regulatory framework that includes all the different forms of regulation.

KEY POINTS IN THIS CHAPTER

■ Integrity and compliance can be perceived as a soft and a hard approach respectively and at opposite ends of a spectrum. Ideally, they should complement each other, as neither, on their own, are sufficient to ensure good standards of conduct.

■ Principles are guides to actions and are built upon values that will guide the ethical behaviour of public officials.

■ There is no general agreement concerning a correct number of principles, although principles concerning accountability, integrity, honesty, impartiality, serving the public interest and obedience to law are universal.

■ Addressing implementation issues is a key factor in ensuring that codes of ethics contribute to good government and the success of implementation will depend upon a number of aspects.

■ Codes of ethics should be subject to review in the light of experience as ethics move on shifting sands and codes need an element of flexibility.

KEY TERMS

■ **Compliance approaches** – the use of laws and regulations to control unethical behaviour.
■ **Integrity approach** – the use of training, education and the integrity of the individual to curb unethical behaviour.
■ **Codes of conduct and ethics** – a rule-based approach to behaviour.
■ **Anti-corruption agencies** – agencies that are created specifically to oversee unethical behaviour and may focus on the investigation of unethical behaviour, the prevention of unethical behaviour or guidance to avoid unethical behaviour or a combination of all three.

INTRODUCTION

No question about it, we're going to have to accustom ourselves to more regulation, but we're going to have to accustom ourselves to the fact that the difference between avarice and self-service and intelligence and public responsibility is not something that yields to the passage of law. This is human behaviour beyond the reach of the law.

(Galbraith 2003: 89)

Galbraith was commenting on the new regimes of compliance following Enron. We have discussed in other chapters the unethical behaviour of public officials in different times and places. The key question is, can we trust public officials to regulate themselves or do we need to introduce regulatory regimes to ensure that our public officials behave themselves? If we do, then what kinds of regimes are needed?

This chapter looks at two tools that have been used to guide and control the behaviour of officials. The first tool is a code of conduct and the second is the creation of an anti-corruption agency. Such tools typically form a compliance approach to regulation and both perform a number of different roles, and we consider these below. Another approach that has been used to guide behaviour and which we examine in detail in the next chapter is the integrity approach, which is concerned with education, training, advice and guidance. Some commentators see integrity and compliance as opposite ends of a spectrum, as a soft approach and a hard approach respectively. We suggest that, in fact, they complement each

95

Table 6.1 A framework of ethical regulation

Policy push	Policy issues	Policy goals	Policy objects	Policy instruments	Policy implementation	Policy styles
1. Critical incidents such as high-profile corruption cases	1. Corruption	1. Punish individuals	1. MPs	1. Laws	1. Leadership	1. Top-down
2. Media pressure	2. Conflicts of interest	2. Stamp out widespread corruption	2. Police	2. Protocols	2. Ethics officer	2. Local variations
3. Citizen pressure	3. Discrimination	3. As a corrective to unethical practices	3. Judges	3. Codes of conduct	3. Training	
4. International law/agencies	4. Nepotism		4. Civil servants	4. Anti-corruption agency	4. Well-trained staff	
			5. Lobbyists			

other and that neither, on their own, is sufficient to ensure good standards of conduct.

We also suggest that none of the tools exist in a policy vacuum and that the policy arena needs to be considered as a backcloth and context that will shape the success, or otherwise, of the tools adopted. We turn our attention, briefly, to this policy arena and suggest a framework in Table 6.1 to locate the policy context consisting of a number of different dimensions:

1. Policy push refers to the factors or critical incidents that might provide the reasons for putting in place an ethical framework. Typically this might include incidents of high profile corruption, or the need to satisfy the demands of donors.
2. Policy issues refer to those that are directly addressed by the introduction of an ethical framework. A key issue is the extent to which the response to the particular issue is proportionate; or establishing a 'sledgehammer to crack a nut'.
3. Policy goals are what the policy is trying to achieve such as curbing corruption, establishing trust, etc.
4. Policy objects refer to individuals or institutions to whom or what the policy is to be applied (e.g. politicians, civil servants, the police, judges or a combination of any of these).
5. Policy instruments refer to the tools that are used to achieve policy goals such as codes of conduct or an anti-corruption agency.
6. Policy implementation, which is crucial, will depend upon leadership and the role of key individuals and adequate resources.
7. Policy styles will reflect the extent of central direction or local discretion and will refer to how policy responses are formulated.

CODES OF CONDUCT

Guidelines and sanctions can take a number of different forms enshrined in rules, regulations, statutes and codes of ethics. It is sometimes the case that codes of ethics, which relate to the ethical conduct of public officials, and codes of conduct, which are wider in scope, covering a range of organizational practices and employee conduct, are distinguished in theory. In practice many organizations use the terms interchangeably and we will follow that practice. However, it is generally considered that, despite the proliferation of codes of ethics for both public and private sector organizations, codes are a necessary but not sufficient instrument to facilitate ethical behaviour. One way of exploring this is by considering codes of ethics as a form of rule-governed activity (see Dawson 1994). Rules can be seen from both an external and an internal point of view (Hart 1960). The external point of view might depict codes as externally imposed, serving instrumental control and followed through fear of sanctions. In contrast, it can be argued that codes need to be embedded within organizations, such that those who fall under the code can take an internal or 'insider' view towards them. Conditions for taking an insider view include trust that others will follow the rules, and general agreement that the rules are a good thing in some sense. These conditions can be facilitated by socialization through ethical training and the generation of trust by the behaviour of role models.

Thus, while agreeing generally with the view that codes are necessary but not sufficient, we argue that a consideration of context, content, implementation and enforcement of codes can enhance their effectiveness, through the adoption of an insider view.

RATIONALE FOR CODES

A number of simple questions can be asked before seeking to develop a code of ethics. These will include, 'What is the problem that a code of ethics seeks to address?' and 'What ethical issues are more amenable to management by ethical rules?' Whatever the scope and content of codes of ethics, it is generally considered that they may perform different functions. They provide a clear statement of ethical values to be aspired to; offer a coherent and consistent set of guidelines to aid the public official; and indicate what sanctions will be imposed where ethical principles are breached. Thus codes of ethics may be aspirational, guiding and regulatory in character. The balance between these three functions will vary depending upon context. Table 6.2 categorizes the functions of codes according to their character.

It is also generally recognized that there are a number of critiques of codes of ethics and that these critiques claim that codes are both too general and too detailed. Thus, it is argued that general statements of values have little operational value and, at the same time, cannot provide guidance in all situations. If they are too detailed they become cumbersome and are not used.

Given the complexity of government activity, it is difficult to construct a code to be applied generally. Codes may conflict with other rules and regulations and may be difficult to enforce. The duties of public officials as outlined in codes may conflict with their rights as individual citizens. Finally, it is suggested that public officials may hide behind the codes and assume that an action that is not explicitly prohibited may be seen as acceptable.

These are serious concerns but they can be overcome with careful drafting, particularly if they are clear, consistent, comprehensive and have practical application. Clarity will aid understanding and minimize ambiguity. Consistency with existing legislation is crucial, as is general agreement upon a set of principles. Inevitably, organizations and governments will have in place a set of disciplinary procedures and will be subject to civil and criminal law. A code of ethics must harmonize with existing legislation and procedures. Similarly, if codes are

Table 6.2 *Functions of codes*

Aspirational

1 Promote public trust and confidence in the ethical performance of public officials
2 Generate pride amongst staff
3 Reaffirm the values of public service to existing public officials and inspire a new generation of public officials
4 Establish external credibility and indicate that ethics are being taken seriously

Guidance

1 Offer a clear statement of values, roles and duties, rights and responsibilities
2 Clarify the ethical behaviour expected of public officials
3 Act as guidelines in developing ethical conduct
4 Form an independent, consistent and pre-determined set of criteria for ethical conduct
5 Help resolve possible ethical dilemmas

Regulatory

1 Clarify procedures and sanctions to deal with misconduct
2 Minimize ambiguity and reduce uncertainty
3 Offer a coherent statement of ethical conduct, drawing together ethical statements which may be scattered throughout different pieces of legislation

underpinned by a set of principles that have been agreed upon by all stakeholders, then consistency will be enhanced. Reference will be made to existing legislation, as far as is known, that governs ethical conduct. Where there are no previous codes it is appropriate to draft the codes as comprehensively as is practicable. They may be amended in the light of experience. Table 6.3 indicates how a set of general principles may be given specific meaning and these may be provided for within a code.

Principles are guides to actions and are built upon values. It is important that there is general agreement amongst key stakeholders on the principles that will guide the ethical behaviour of public officials. However, there is no general agreement concerning a correct number of principles, although principles concerning accountability, integrity, honesty, impartiality, serving the public interest and obedience to law are universal. For example:

1. The seven principles of the Nolan Committee in the UK are selflessness, integrity, objectivity, accountability, openness, honesty and leadership.
2. The principles chosen by the US government include loyalty, public duty, honesty, impartiality, obedience to law and fairness.

Table 6.3 *Principles in practice*

Principles	In practice
1. Integrity	1. Personal conduct 2. Carrying out duties 3. Professional competence, demonstrating skill, care, efficiency and effectiveness 4. Maintaining and enhancing the reputation of government 5. Demonstrating goodwill and energy 6. Preserving public trust and confidence

2. Loyalty	1. The scope of loyalty
	   – Constitution
	   – Government/ministers
	   – Superiors
	   – Colleagues
	   – Family and friends
	   – Others
	2. Outside employment
	3. Post employment
	4. Justifying 'disloyal' behaviour – whistle-blowing
	5. Misplaced loyalties

3. Transparency	1. Access for citizens 2. Focus on processes and outcomes 3. Performance evaluation and feedback 4. Providing basic information 5. Procedures for redress 6. Enhancing democracy 7. Register of interests 8. Transparency in public procurement 9. Publicizing government services 10. Recognizing the importance of public scrutiny
4. Confidentiality	1. Rules on disclosure 2. Misuse of information for personal gain 3. Advice given to ministers 4. Criteria for non-release of information 5. Confidential information in public procurement
5. Honesty	1. Enhancing trust in the decisions and actions of public officials 2. Exhibiting truthfulness with relevant stakeholders 3. Bribes and fraud 5. Declaration of gifts and hospitality 6. Dishonest use of time, equipment and financial resources 7. Misuse of allowances
6. Accountability	1. Specification of accountable to whom, for what, and in what form 2. Taking responsibility 3. Accountability mechanisms 4. Use of discretion 5. Financial, administrative, management, performance and legal accountabilities

Table 6.3 *Continued*

Principles	In practice
7. Serving the public interest	1. Conflicts of interest 2. Registering relevant interests and assets 3. Identifying those public officials for who register of interests is appropriate, e.g. those dealing with taxes, housing, the issuing of permits or licences or in other areas where public demand exceeds supply 4. Declarations of interest 5. Identifying circumstances where public duty might be subverted by the pursuit of private interests of the public official or others
8. Exercising legitimate authority	1. Abuse of public office for private gain 2. Handing out of favours, including nepotism 3. Defining inappropriate, unauthorized or illegal actions 4. Exercising authority unfairly or with discrimination 5. Abusing the rights of others 6. Judicious use of resources, not abusing government property 7. Not interfering improperly with the judiciary or the legislature
9. Impartiality	1. The duty to offer impartial advice based on facts, without 'fear or favour' to different groups of stakeholders including ministers and clients 2. Adhering to non-discriminatory practices 3. The merit principle in recruitment and promotion 4. Consider the views of all relevant stakeholders when making decisions, as far as is practicable 5. The political activities of civil servants
10. Respecting the law	1. Respecting the Constitution and the law 2. Accepting the supremacy of law 3. Acting according to the law 4. Guidelines when asked to break the law
11. Responsiveness	1. Balancing responsiveness with other principles such as accountabilities 2. Respecting, and responding to, the rights and expectations of others 3. Responding to others with courtesy and being sensitive to their needs 4. Advertising grievance procedures
12. Exercising leadership	1. Example setting and acting ethically at all times 2. Taking the lead in endorsing and implementing ethical principles 3. Demonstrating leadership in the public interest 4. Demonstrating consistency in the application of principles 5. Communicating realistic expectations to staff 6. Developing a culture of openness and building and maintaining trust

3. The 12 principles chosen by the OECD are concerned with leadership, accountability, transparency, relations with the private sector, the duties and rights of public officials, standards and guidance.
4. The principles in New Zealand are concerned with integrity, professionalism, lawful obligations, honesty, loyalty, efficiency and respecting the rights of others.

Whatever the agreed-upon set of principles chosen they will be applicable to all groups, although how they are applied will vary. The principles chosen should form the basis of ethical conduct and it is considered that they should be positive rather than negative in tone. The set of principles in Table 6.3 describes values to be aspired to by all public officials. They are, by design, general in nature. However, it is recognized that more needs to be provided to guide public officials in their day-to-day activities and that the principles need to be grounded in actual experience. Thus, each of the principles needs to be taken in turn, concrete issues identified and guidance offered on how these issues can be resolved. It is likely that there will be both similarities and differences in the issues raised for each group of public officials. Yet, it is worth noting that many countries do not attempt to draw up different codes for different groups of public officials.

INTERNATIONAL PRACTICE

The adoption of codes of ethics has long been a practice amongst governments worldwide and these codes have taken a number of different forms, varying in terms of scope, content, intention, status and application. There has also been a recent impetus behind the codification of ethical behaviour as the need to restate traditional values in a rapidly changing public services environment has become obvious.

Kernaghan (1980) describes codes as located on a continuum between the two polar extremes of a 'Ten Commandments' approach (e.g. The Nolan Committee principles) to a Justinian Code model (e.g. the Australian Public Service Values and Code of Conduct). The Ten Commandments approach contains a limited number of principles or values that are expressed in broad terms. Examples of this approach are the seven principles advocated by the Nolan Committee (1994) in the UK or the 12 principles enshrined in the OECD (1996). The Justinian Code model, extremely detailed and comprehensive in scope, might be exemplified by the Australian Public Service Values and Code of Conduct. This document covers public service values and a code of conduct in the same document and is 88 pages in length in 17 chapters. The chapters are grouped under four main headings: Relations with Government and Parliament, Relations with the Public, Relations in the Workplace and Personal Behaviour.

In contrast, the code of conduct for the New Zealand public service originally established three principles of public service and then illustrated how these might be applied in a seven-page document. The code of conduct has now been reduced to one page. The OECD (1996) distinguished between compliance-based systems and integrity-based systems. Integrity-based systems define overall aspirational values and focus on encouraging good behaviour, while compliance-based systems focus on strict compliance with detailed rules, often defined in legislation, indicating the sort of behaviour that can be avoided. There are a number of factors that will determine the approach adopted and these include:

1. The extent to which there is in place a clear ethics infrastructure. Where such an infrastructure is not in place the tendency is to follow the rules-based approach.
2. The extent to which there is a tradition of public sector values, agreed upon by all stakeholders.
3. The strength of administrative and legal traditions. Until recently, the UK Civil Service did not feel the need to codify public service values as it was assumed that these would be passed down from one generation of civil servants to the next.
4. The impact of public management reforms in terms of increasing commercialization, devolved responsibility, the introduction of business practices, closer engagement with the private sector and increased expectations on the part of citizens.
5. The existence, and strength, of other forms of control such as internal and external audit.
6. The extent, and pace, of economic modernization.
7. The strength of civil society and relationships between different branches of government and the existence of a free press.

The OECD finds that there is a growing emphasis on broader guidance rather than detailed control, partly as a result of the impact of public sector management reforms, which have moved from rules-based public administration to results-based public management. However, it has long been considered that in the results-based approach there is a danger that traditional values of probity and integrity may be forgotten in the clamour to be more business-like (see Lawton 1998).

Where there is a lack of a systematic approach to public sector ethics or the non-existence of a coherent set of principles to guide the behaviour of public officials it is appropriate to adopt codes that address both the integrity and the compliance-based approaches. Integrity-based approaches tend to be too general and they are difficult to enforce. However, they do set out a clear set of ethical principles and define what constitutes good behaviour.

Compliance-based approaches tend to be too detailed and cumbersome, leading to inefficiency. Such an approach encourages too strict an adherence to a formal set of rules. Notably, the complexity of government makes it difficult to legislate

103

for every possible issue or course of action. Not only that, but this approach encourages public officials to hide behind formal rules and does not encourage them to exercise ethical judgement. It is important to recognize that in a rapidly changing external environment formal rules cannot cover every contingency and that public officials will need to exercise judgement. This judgement can be developed through commitment to a set of general principles and ethical training.

It is recognized, however, that critical judgement needs to be supplemented by guidelines and the codes of ethics provide practical guidance based upon general principles. It is, therefore, argued that the codes of ethics will encourage good behaviour based on a set of general principles (the integrity approach) and will offer practical guidance based on these principles, indicating penalties for breaches of these principles (the compliance approach).

THE CONTENT OF THE CODES

To some extent, the content of the codes will reflect the particular circumstances of individual countries. For example, in those countries such as the UK or Australia, where much of the work of the public services has been contracted out, then relationships with the contractors and possible conflicts of interest have featured strongly. In other countries where there is a tradition of movement of individuals between the public and private sectors as in the 'revolving doors' that characterize bureaucrats in the US, then post-employment issues are prominent. In developing countries characterized by a traditional society, how to overcome patronage and nepotism based on strong kinship or ethnic ties is an issue.

Notwithstanding these differences, there is a range of issues that appear to be universal in nature even though they may take slightly different forms in individual countries. These will include:

— standards of conduct of public officials
— disclosure of official information
— the political neutrality of public officials and engagement in political activity
— relationships between the relevant stakeholders of civil servants, elected representatives, ministers, the judiciary, citizens generally, clients and interest groups
— conflicts of interest and balancing competing loyalties
— hospitality and gifts
— corruption and fraud
— duties and rights of public officials
— disclosure and Registers of Interests
— employment matters in terms of recruitment and promotion on merit, not patronage

- maladministration, which includes giving out misleading information, depriving individuals of their rights, or administering services in an inequitable manner
- misuse of power
- discrimination, malice or bias
- whistle-blowing
- post-employment issues.

The formulation and delivery of government policy requires the interaction of a number of different stakeholders engaging in different relationships with each other. Although it is recognized that a number of codes are required, it is also the case that these codes do not exist in isolation from each other and that the codes will need to address the nature of the relationships between the different groups of stakeholders. For example, civil servants will have obligations to their minister and the minister will, likewise, have duties to the civil service even though they will be governed by different codes.

Formulating public policy and delivering public services is an increasingly complex business. The competing demands on those who formulate policy and deliver services are increasing and it is recognized that the task of the public official is not an easy one.

IMPLEMENTATION OF THE CODES

Addressing implementation issues is a key factor in ensuring that codes of ethics contribute to good government. The success of implementation will depend upon a number of factors including:

1. The public commitment to an ethical public service must be demonstrated by those in leadership positions, whether political, administrative or judicial. Without that commitment the proposals will not be taken seriously.
2. The extent to which ethical principles become embedded in organizational culture will be important in determining the success of implementation. This will take time but it can be achieved in a number of ways including:

    (i) consulting with key stakeholders in the development of the codes of ethics
    (ii) disseminating and publicizing the codes through workshops and briefings to those who will fall under their remit
    (iii) ensuring that the ethical principles form part of the induction programme for all categories of public officials
    (iv) demonstrating the benefits of an ethical public service to public officials and to the public interest as a whole.

3. The extent of flexibility and diversity of codes will influence the effectiveness of implementation. Some staff may, for example, see the codes as just another control mechanism imposed by senior officials. It is important, therefore, that the aspirational and guiding characteristics of the codes are stressed as much as the regulatory requirements.

The codes of ethics should not be written in 'tablets of stone', but should be subject to review in the light of experience in, say five years. Ethics moves on shifting sands and codes of ethics need an element of flexibility.

ENFORCEMENT

Without enforcement, simply setting limits on behaviour and threatening sanctions is like having teeth without biting. The threat of sanctions will only act as a deterrent where they are sufficient, enforced and respected. Enforcement begins with an assessment of the incentives and disincentives to proscribed behaviour, backed up by independent and adequately resourced prosecution and investigation services. These services need to be seen as being effective to gain credibility, not only in the public service but also in the public at large.

(OECD 1996: 32)

It is important to strike a balance between encouraging good conduct and policing behaviour. This balance will vary from country to country and over time. The most effective enforcement mechanisms involve a mixture of law enforcement, independent investigative bodies, preventative management controls, transparency mechanisms and raising awareness and developing skills. It is important to note that in many countries the ethical conduct of public officials is governed by more than one piece of legislation. For example, the US has passed the Ethics in Government Act (1978), Inspector General Act (1978), Ethics Reform Act (1989) and the Lobbying Disclosure Act (1995). Other countries, in addition, also have Freedom of Information Acts and whistle-blowing legislation. Ethical issues for public officials constantly evolve, and to seek to legislate for all acts of unethical behaviour requires an ever-increasing number of statutes, or the constant revision of existing statute. The codes of ethics will include existing statute. The codes will also recognize new categories of inappropriate, unethical and illegal behaviour and will include relevant guidelines. It is important to recognize that the codes should not be considered final and 'set in stone'. It is likely that as the political, social and economic environment changes then new demands will be placed upon public officials and guidelines will need to be introduced to aid public officials in their decision-making. However, all codes of ethics need to address three questions: What type of offence is it? What sanctions should be imposed? Who is to impose those sanctions?

1. The type of offence

Breaches of conduct are usually characterized in terms of illegal behaviour, unethical behaviour or inappropriate or unreasonable behaviour. It is recognized, however, that the boundaries between these different types of behaviour are blurred.

The OECD (1996) defines these different types of behaviour as follows:

1. Illegal behaviour – acts that are against the law; may cover criminal offences to misdemeanours.
2. Unethical behaviour – acts that are against ethical guidelines, principles or values.
3. Inappropriate behaviour – acts that are against normal convention or practice.

2. Appropriate sanctions

It is considered that punishment by the courts may be too blunt an instrument to apply to all types of unethical or inappropriate practices. Sanctions should be appropriate to the offence. As indicated above, there will be in existence a body of relevant law and disciplinary procedures. Regulating unethical or inappropriate behaviour is more difficult but guidelines are more flexible and easier to amend than law. It is proposed that the sanctions be reviewed in, say, two years, to evaluate their effects. It is appropriate to identify a minimum and a maximum sanction for all breaches of the codes. Undoubtedly, judgement will have to be exercised by the relevant disciplinary authority.

3. Enforcing bodies

A key question is who is to enforce the different types of sanctions. Often breaches of conduct are dealt with either by the courts or through disciplinary action. Many countries have the office of ombudsman and a central body dealing with fraud and corruption. The terms of reference, duties and powers of these bodies need to be absolutely clear and discrete. It will thus be possible to clearly identify what sanctions are to be imposed for what breaches of conduct and by what authority. Thus, each code of ethics may include a matrix based on the example in Table 6.4.

Table 6.5 identifies the range of sanctions that might be appropriate.

Codes of ethics are necessary but not sufficient in themselves in the pursuit of good governance. They must form part of a wider ethical framework which is itself part of a wider framework of public service reform, including the development of a human resources strategy and a service delivery strategy. Other elements in the framework will include ethical training and education; strengthening internal and external accountability mechanisms, particularly financial ones; and developing skills and increasing knowledge. We recognize that unethical practices can result

Table 6.4 *Disciplinary matrix*

Type of offence	Appropriate sanctions	Enforced by
Inappropriate	Reprimand, disciplinary action	Superiors, public service tribunal, ombudsman
Unethical	Disciplinary action, dismissal, the law	Public service tribunal, central body, the courts
Illegal	The law	Central body, the courts

Table 6.5 *Types of sanction*

Sanction	Type of sanction	Seriousness of offence
1. Verbal warning	Administrative	Low
2. Written warning	Administrative	Low
3. Fine	Administrative	Medium
4. Disallowing of next increment	Administrative	Medium
5. Downgrading	Administrative	Medium
6. Dismissal	Administrative	Serious
7. Fine	Criminal	Serious
8. Imprisonment	Criminal	Serious

from ignorance and incompetence, for example, not processing welfare claims in time, leading to unnecessary hardship.

We have argued for a balanced approach to developing codes of ethics that can inspire public officials, offer guidance and regulate behaviour. In so doing any code will need to include a set of principles that are operationalized for different types of public officials and different functional departments. There will thus be a balance between the general and the specific, comprehensive and selective, national and local. A code of ethics will also need to be in harmony with existing disciplinary procedures and legislation. Indeed one feature of a code could be that it brings together all sanctions under one document. Of course codes, in offering guidance, should not minimize individual ethical responsibility nor offer a shield behind which individuals can hide. The key is ethical judgement of which codes play a part in developing. Not all ethical issues lend themselves easily to rules or sanctions; ethical judgement is required when making a decision. Rules can function as shortcuts to decision-making but rules do assume that different situations have enough in common to be treated as a coherent group.

Building codes from the bottom-up will help in developing that judgement since the process of code development itself is educative. Formulation and implementation are but two sides of the same coin and can be considered alongside each other. Developing codes from the bottom-up will help develop an 'insider' perspective and minimize the key problem of codes being seen as a management control tool imposed from above.

ANTI-CORRUPTION AGENCIES (ACAs)

One response, globally, to the unethical conduct of public officials has been to create an anti-corruption agency (ACA) to address the problems. In Africa, Europe, Australasia, Latin America and Asia there are numerous examples of such bodies and we discuss a number of these below. In general such bodies perform a number of different tasks, some bodies include all of these tasks, while others might have a more limited role. The key tasks will include:

1. Receive and respond to complaints concerning breaches of the law, rules and regulations, including codes of conduct.
2. Administering registers of interest and asset declaration.
3. Investigation of complaints.
4. Prosecutions and imposing sanctions.
5. Research and analysis, leading to dissemination of good practice.
6. Preventative measures in terms of ethics training, guidance and support, public information, education and community engagement.

As their names suggest, the initial reasons for creating such agencies are concerned with examples of corruption by public officials. Corruption itself has been studied by economists, political scientists, philosophers, public administrators, and business and management scholars, and there are numerous definitions of corruption. For the sake of simplicity we use the same definition of corruption as Transparency International (TI), the leading non-governmental organization in the field. They define corruption on their website as 'the abuse of entrusted power for private gain. It hurts everyone who depends on the integrity of people in a position of authority' (http://www.transparency.org/). Most scholars use the principal agent model in their discussion of corruption. That is, corruption occurs when an agent betrays the principal's interests to further their own interest and this is made possible by the information asymmetry between the two groups. The principal could be politicians or citizens generally and the agent will be either civil servants or politicians. Thus, to limit corruption it would be necessary to reduce the level of discretion of agents, limit their monopoly of information and enhance accountability mechanisms. It is assumed that the principal wants to curb corruption in their role as guardians of the public purse. Yet who guards the guardians? If the principals themselves are corrupt then the principal/agent model of corruption may not be relevant. The propensity for corruption has been expressed as a formula:

$$C = M + D - A$$

Where corruption (C) is a function of monopoly power (M) plus discretion by officials (D) minus accountability (A) (Klitgaard 1998).

TYPES OF ACAs

The type of regulator will reflect the regulatory environment at large. For example, some countries may be characterized by an adversarial style of regulation, with strict laws of investigation and stricter enforcement. In the UK, the regulatory style is more benign with a 'soft touch' approach in evidence. Similarly, the regulatory style will reflect a view on whether regulation should be based upon internal motivation and peer review rather than control. Indeed, the integrity bureau for the city of Amsterdam takes the former view and much of its work involves training (Huberts, Six and Lasthuizen 2008).

Four models of anti-corruption agencies have been identified (Heilbrunn 2004; Quah 2007):

1. The universal model with powers of investigation, prevention and communi-cation such as the Hong Kong Independent Commission Against Corruption (ICAC) created in 1974. This model has been copied around the world but, often, with less success.
2. The investigative model involving a small centralized investigative commission such as the Singapore CPIB established in 1952. This model, although more limited in scope, is very focused.
3. The parliamentary model that reports to parliamentary committees and is independent from the executive and judicial branches of government. The New South Wales Independent Commission Against Corruption (ICAC), based in Sydney, is an example of this model.
4. The multi-agency model that weaves together a number of agencies (e.g. US Office of Government Ethics (OGE) works with the Justice department).

The success of the Hong Kong ICAC and the Singapore CPIB is reflected in Transparency International's Corruption Perception Index. This index ranks countries and territories in a league table based upon how corrupt their public sector is perceived to be. Out of 182 countries, Singapore is ranked fifth and Hong Kong twelfth. New Zealand is ranked the least corrupt and Somalia the most corrupt.

Table 6.6 Different kinds of agencies

	Standards for England	Hong Kong ICAC	Office of Government Ethics (US)
When formed and why	2001 in response to high profile scandals in English local government	1974, widespread corruption in police	1978 following Watergate scandal
Staffing	80 approximately (2009)	1,300 including 600 investigators	80
Budget	£7.8m (2009)	$90m HK pa	$14m US
Functions	Issue guidance on a code of conduct and to investigate complaints against breaches of the code	Enforcement, prevention, education, community	Develops ethics rules and regulations, provides guidance, evaluate departmental ethics programmes, advise on conflicts of interest
Scope	Limited to local government politicians	Extensive and includes private sector	Limited to advise
Relationship with government	Independent, but Board appointed by relevant minister	Independent	Director appointed by president
Powers	Investigation, advice, guidance	Enforcement, prevention, education	Limited
Standing	Mixed support from major political parties leading to its abolition in 2012	Highly regarded and a model for other agencies	Highly regarded

Generally such bodies are created in response to deep-lying corruption, often in the police force. The key question is the extent to which ethical failure is systemic throughout the whole organization. Table 6.6 illustrates the different kinds of agencies.

A focus on corruption is at one end of a spectrum of regulatory functions. At the other end will be a focus on softer issues such as 'respect for persons' or 'bringing the organization into disrepute'. Standards for England are located towards this end of the spectrum. Different issues may, therefore, require different regulatory regimes. The Hong Kong ICAC was set up to combat corruption and pursued a three-pronged approach involving prevention, punishment and promotion of an ethical agenda. Not only that but the remit of the Hong Kong ICAC covers both public and private sector organizations, and the remit of Standards for England is to focus on one group alone: local authority politicians. The educational/ promotional role of the Hong Kong ICAC is important to reconcile State and society values. The critical success factors of the Hong Kong ICAC have been described by former Commissioner Fanny Law (2008) as:

–   the independence of the agency
–   wide-ranging investigative powers backed by statute, but subject to internal and external oversight
–   dedicated and professional staff
–   three-pronged approach involving investigation, prevention and education
–   public support
–   active participation in international and regional fora to update knowledge and enhance co-operation.

We might also add political will and support. Other commentators also include a mixture of internal and external factors: operational issues such as adequate financial resources and skilled staff; that it is subject to review by a free press and civil society; that it is accountable to the public and is lead, and staffed, with integrity; has access to documentation and the power to question witnesses. Externally it will also help if there is economic and political stability and a focus on reducing incentives and opportunities for corruption, appropriate legal frameworks and is situated in a comprehensive anti-corruption strategy supported by effective and complementary bodies.

In practice it is difficult to find such ideal conditions. Quah (2008), for example, argues that India's anti-corruption strategy has been ineffective, partly due to the lack of political will of its leaders and that curbing corruption in India in the foreseeable future is highly unlikely. He refers to government monopoly in the supply of goods and services and lack of competition, discretion in decision-making, lack of accountability to citizens, and information being available to providers but not to citizens. India ranks ninety-fifth on the TI Corruption Perception Index (discussed above), and it is getting worse. Critics of anti-corruption agencies in Africa (e.g. Doig, Watt and Williams 2007) point to the absence of building blocks such as an old-fashioned reliable civil service, and the lack of funding and adequate staffing. Meagher (2005) argues that short-term success is possible but is difficult to sustain in a dysfunctional environment of political instability and disorder. The tension between ethics and politics is clearly evident in the success or otherwise of ACAs; without political commitment, or even worse, the exploitation of such agencies by political parties or individual politicians for their own ends, then the credibility of ACAs is shattered. Similarly, such agencies cannot survive as 'islands of integrity' surrounded by a sea of government corruption. At the same time, ethics will need to be supported by law as the legal powers of ACAs will need to be clear and unambiguous and enforceable through prosecutors and judges acting with integrity. Also, as we discuss in Chapter 8 on ethical performance, there will be implementation issues involving adequate staffing and funding, clear objectives and communication strategies and so on (see Persson, Rothstein and Teorell 2010). Thus the critical success factors of ACAs will include:

External

1. Comprehensive anti-corruption legislation
2. Legal tools to support investigations
3. Independence from political interference
4. An oversight committee to 'guard the guardians'.

Internal

5. Adequate staff funding
6. Cut red tape to minimize opportunities for corruption
7. Reduce opportunities for corruption in those agencies that have access to the public such as public works, internal revenue, customs, the police
8. Punish the guilty to make corruption a high-risk, low-reward activity
9. Clear reporting and accountability lines.

Transparency International has adopted a holistic approach to corruption and makes use of the concept of the National Integrity System (NIS), which has been developed and promoted by TI as part of its approach to countering corruption. The NIS consists of the principal institutions and actors that contribute to integrity, transparency and accountability in a society. See Figure 6.1, National integrity system.

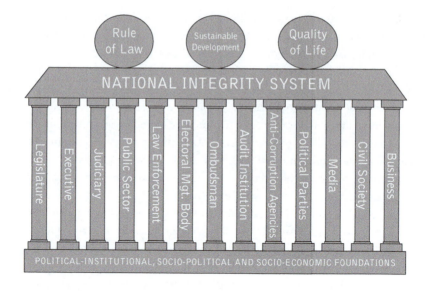

Figure 6.1 *National integrity system*

For TI, strengthening the NIS promotes better governance across all aspects of society and, ultimately, contributes to a more just society overall, as depicted in the NIS temple.

CONCLUSIONS

We have suggested that the relationships between ethics, politics and the law come into sharp relief when examining compliance measures, recognizing how difficult it is to find clear distance between them. This chapter has focused on two tools that have been used to combat unethical practices: codes of conduct and anti-corruption agencies (ACAs); and it is generally considered that, while they are necessary, they are not sufficient in themselves and will need extra measures taken, and it is to these that we turn in the next chapter.

REFERENCES

Doig, A., Watt, D. and Williams, R. (2007) 'Why Do developing Country Anti-corruption Commissions Fail To Deal With Corruption? Understanding the Three Dilemmas of Organizational Development, Performance Expectation, and Donor and Government Cycles', *Public Administration and Development* 27 (3): 251–9.

Dawson, A.J. (1994) 'Professional Codes of Practice and Ethical Conduct', *Journal of Applied Philosophy* 11 (2): 145–53.

Galbraith, J.K. (2003) 'Concerning Enronism' in Terkel, S. *Hope Dies Last: Keeping the Faith in Difficult Times*. New York: The New Press, pp. 87–90.

Hart, H.L.A. (1960) *The Concept of Law*. Oxford: Clarendon Press.

Heilbrunn, J.R. (2004) *Anti-Corruption Commissions: Panacea or Real Medicine to Fight Corruption?* Washington, DC: The World Bank.

Huberts, L., Six, F.E. and Lasthuizen, K. (2008) 'Evaluation of the Amsterdam Integrity System' in Huberts, L.W.J.C., Anechiarico, F. and Six, F.E. (eds) *Local Integrity Systems: Fighting Corruption and Safeguarding Integrity in Seven World Cities*. The Hague: BJu Legal Publishers, pp. 211–27.

Kernaghan, K. (1980) 'Codes of Ethics and Public Administration: Progress, Problems and Prospects', *Canadian Public Administration* 30: 331–51.

Klitgaard, R. (1988) *Controlling Corruption*. Berkeley and Los Angeles, CA: University of California Press.

Law, F. (2008) 'The Hong Kong Integrity System' in Huberts, L.W.J.C., Anechiarico, F. and Six, F.E. (eds) *Local Integrity Systems: Fighting Corruption and Safeguarding Integrity in Seven World Cities*. The Hague: BJu Legal Publishers, pp. 79–104.

Lawton, A. (1998) 'Business Practices and the Public Service Ethos' in Sampford, C., Preston, N. and Bois, C.-A. (eds) *Public Sector Ethics: Finding and Implementing Values*. Annandale, NSW: Federation Press/Routledge, pp. 53–67.

Meagher, P. (2005) 'Anti-corruption Agencies: Rhetoric Versus Reality', *The Journal of Policy Reform* 8 (1): 69–103.

OECD (1996) *Ethics in the Public Service: Current Issues and Practice*. Paris: OECD.

Sherman, T. (1998) 'Public Sector Ethics: Prospects and Challenges' in Sampford, C., Preston, N. and Bois, C.-A. (eds) *Public Sector Ethics: Finding and Implementing Values*. Annandale, NSW: Federation Press/Routledge, pp. 13–25.

Persson, A., Rothstein, B. and Teorell, J. (2010) 'The Failure of Anti-corruption Policies: A Theoretical Mischaracterization of the Problem', QoG Working Paper Series 2010:19. The Quality of Government Institute, University of Gothenburg, Sweden.

Quah, J.S.T. (2007). *Combating Corruption Singapore-Style: Lessons for Other Asian Countries*. Volume 2 in the Maryland Series in Contemporary Asian Studies. Baltimore, MD: University of Maryland School of Law.

Quah, J.S.T. (2008) 'Curbing Corruption in India: An Impossible Dream?' *Asian Journal of Political Science* 16 (3): 240–59.

Chapter 7

Integrity approaches
Can we trust public officials to regulate themselves?

LEARNING OBJECTIVES

By the end of this chapter you should:

■ be able to describe the nature of ethical guidance by means of an integrity approach and informal controls
■ be able to describe the differences between a compliance and an integrity approach to organizational ethics
■ be able to solve an ethical dilemma by using an ethical decision-making model
■ be able to consider the success factors of training and education in developing the ethical reasoning and decision-making of employees.

KEY POINTS IN THIS CHAPTER

■ Integrity and compliance can be perceived as a soft and a hard approach, respectively, and at opposite ends of a spectrum. Ideally, they should complement each other as neither, on their own, are sufficient to ensure good standards of conduct.
■ An integrity approach uses internal controls and a compliance approach uses external controls in order to operate as an ethical organization. The integrity approach is assumed to be more effective.
■ Building on Chapter 2, an ethical decision-making model can be used to help individuals and groups of individuals in organizations to analyze ethical dilemmas they are faced with in daily practice.
■ Ethical dilemma training can have different purposes and depends on several success factors to be an effective means for enhancing ethical decision-making of public officials.

KEY TERMS

- **Compliance approaches** – the use of external controls to control unethical behaviour, for example, laws and regulations.
- **Integrity approaches** – the use of internal controls to stimulate ethical behaviour, for example, training, education and the integrity of the individual.
- **Responsibility** – objective responsibility, i.e. accountability and obligation, are expectations from external stakeholders towards civil servants, while subjective responsibility is one's own feeling towards the duty.
- **External controls** – imposed, top-down instruments to steer employee ethical conduct.
- **Internal controls** – instruments that aim to internalize moral values and foster employee ethical conduct.
- **Ethical dilemma** – a situation of conflicting responsibilities in which you have to make a difficult choice between two sets of moral expectations or values that seem incompatible, and neither alternative is without significant costs.
- **Ethical decision-making model** – a pragmatic and systematic way of reasoning to help you solve an ethical dilemma.

INTRODUCTION

> Creating an organization that encourages exemplary conduct may be the best way to prevent damaging misconduct.
>
> (Paine 1994: 87–90)

In the previous chapter we described the compliance approach to organizational ethics. Two instruments, codes of conduct and anti-corruption agencies, were discussed for their use in guiding and controlling the behaviour of officials. In this chapter we will investigate integrity or values-based approaches to organizational ethics and the role it potentially plays in fostering an ethical climate in public sector organizations. Although the integrity approach has a different orientation and is designed for different goals than the compliance approach, both can enforce each other and should therefore ideally complement each other. They key aim of this chapter is to gain a greater understanding of the underlying rationale of the integrity approach; that is, when it comes to organizational ethics, civil servants should be able to make ethical decisions autonomously based on sound ethical arguments and considerations, and be intrinsically motivated to 'do the right thing' (see above citation). This chapter therefore builds on our introduction to ethical decision-making in Chapter 2 and elaborates on an ethical decision-making model, often used in ethics training and education, which helps officials in a practical way to reflect on ethical issues and solve ethical dilemmas. Exercises are included here to provide some training in ethical decision-making and thereby deepening your understanding of the overall aim of an integrity approach to organizational ethics.

COMPLIANCE VERSUS INTEGRITY APPROACHES

John Rohr (1989) was one of the first scholars who made a clear distinction between a compliance or rule-based, and an integrity or values-based approach, between the 'low road' of compliance and the 'high road' of integrity. Paine (1994), in her contribution to the *Harvard Business Review*, also developed this distinction. As outlined in the previous chapter, she described the compliance approach as a rule-based or legal strategy to organizational ethics, which focuses on the prevention of unethical conduct by detecting integrity violations and sanctioning employees who transgress the law, rules and/or organizational norms. 'Such programmes tend to emphasize the prevention of unlawful conduct, primarily by increasing surveillance and control and by imposing penalties for wrongdoers' (Paine 1994: 109).

Organizations that follow a compliance approach are mainly concerned with avoiding legal sanctions and conceive ethics as 'that what is legal and within the law'.

The integrity approach reflects an opposite vision on organizational ethics. Programmes within this type of approach aim to define organizational (moral) values and encourage employee commitment to act upon these leading values and ethical aspirations (Treviño *et al*. 1999). An integrity approach is based on the concept of self-governance of employees in accordance with a set of guiding principles within the organization and the wider environment. An important role in this strategy to organizational ethics is played by managers, a point we return to in Chapter 9 on ethical leadership.

According to many scholars, compliance approaches might be counterproductive because they emphasize avoiding punishment instead of promoting self-governance. Ethics is defined in terms of legal compliance rather than ethical aspirations, and they implicitly endorse a code of moral mediocrity (Paine 1994). In practice, relying on anti-corruption enforcement alone may not lead to success, as countries have turned increasingly to institutionalized integrity management, relying more on preventative measures, for example China (Gong 2011). A values-based approach could be more effective because it is rooted in self-governance and because it is more likely to motivate employees to behave in accordance with shared values, thereby leading to a 'do-it-right' climate (Paine 1994: 113). Treviño and associates (1999) conducted a large-scale survey within business organizations to find out 'what works and what hurts' in managing ethics and legal compliance. Their results indicated that the choice of either an integrity approach or a compliance approach for an organizational integrity policy matters for the degree and sort of effects that policies have on the ethical awareness, the attitudes and behaviour of employees.

Moreover, the policy orientation and especially the perceived follow-through (i.e. consistency in word and actions) seemed even more important than the formal characteristics and instruments of the chosen integrity policy. Furthermore, their research showed that a solid ethical culture is crucial to organizational ethics, which includes ethical leadership, fair treatment of employees and the integration of ethics in discussions and decision-making. They conclude that although both compliance and integrity programmes can be effective and can complement each other, an integrity approach is more successful and has more positive outcomes, mainly because it aims at building an ethical culture.

Before continuing and giving details about integrity approaches and their related instruments, consider Box 7.1 and try to answer the discussion questions.

BOX 7.1   THE INTEGRITY VS. COMPLIANCE APPROACH

'A strategy based on integrity holds organizations to a more robust standard. While compliance is rooted in avoiding legal sanctions, organizational integrity is based on the concept of self-governance in accordance with a set of guiding principles. From the perspective of integrity, the task of ethics management is to define and give life to an organization's guiding values, to create an environment that supports ethically sound behaviour, and to instil a sense of shared accountability among employees ... Designed by corporate counsel, the goal of compliance-based ethics programs is to prevent, detect, and punish legal violations ... But organizational ethics means more than avoiding illegal practice; and providing employees with a rule book will do little to address the problems underlying unlawful conduct ... [Therefore] managers would be mistaken to regard legal compliance as an adequate means for addressing the full range of ethical issues that arise every day ... An integrity strategy is broader, deeper, and more demanding than a legal compliance.'

Source: Paine (1994: 106, 109, 111)

Discussion questions

■ In which ways do you think an integrity or values strategy or approach is 'broader, deeper and more demanding' than a (legal) compliance approach? Give examples to illustrate this.

■ The compliance or rule-based approach is considered to be rooted in avoiding legal sanctions, thereby reflecting the idea that '*if it's legal, it's ethical*'. Think of a situation/scenario/case in which legal compliance (i.e. action and behaviour that is in line with the law) is necessary, but not sufficient in order to meet ethical standards and reflect ethical values.

■ Consider potential pitfalls of the concept of self-governance that underlies the integrity or values approach. Having identified (some of) these pitfalls, think of criteria and conditions that need to be met in order to transform the theoretical concept of self-governance into a realistic and successful *modus operandi* within organizations.

So far it has become clear that compliance and integrity approaches have different orientations with regard to ethics, goals and underlying behavioural assumptions. Likewise, in both approaches a diverse range of policies, methods and instruments is available from which to choose. Cooper (2006) distinguishes external and internal controls, which can be employed to foster responsible behaviour in organizations. External controls are imposed, top-down instruments to steer employee ethical conduct, such as laws, rules and codes, and monitoring and reinforcement of such rules by sanctioning wrongdoers. External controls fit with the compliance approach. Internal controls are instruments that aim to internalize moral values to foster employee ethical conduct, such as ethical dilemma training, exchange of information and experiences, and/or reinforcement by rewarding exemplary behaviour. Also ethical leadership and the fostering of an ethical culture and climate are important ways to accomplish desired behaviour of employees. Internal controls are important instruments within an integrity approach. The orientation and policies are reflected in the implementation of both ethics strategies – in the standards, leadership and staffing, activities and the emphasis on education and training. These main differences are summarized in Table 7.1. Nevertheless, it is important to keep in mind that many organizations use a mix of approaches and instruments, although Geuras and Garofalo (2005) also note that still many public organizations do not have a consistent approach to ethics at all.

More broadly, we might ask if the organization itself sustains a moral community. In order to answer that question we could look at the different components of an organization and think about these in terms of ethics. For example, is the structure of the organization hierarchical with all power located at the top, or is it flatter with appropriate decision-making powers at the appropriate levels (Jaques 1990)? Or is leadership of the organization drawn from one privileged small cross-section of the population or are there opportunities for women and minority groups to break through the 'glass ceiling'? Do recruitment and promotion criteria reflect and reward ethical behaviour as well as rewarding efficient and effective behaviour? Are accountability mechanisms clear and transparent?

Now consider the job dilemma in Exercise 7.1. How do organizational ethics programmes influence employee behaviour and which do you think would be more effective?

Table 7.1 Different approaches

Orientation	Integrity approach	Compliance approach
Ethics	Self-governance and subjective responsibility according to chosen standards within organizations	Conformity with externally imposed standards and objective responsibilities
Aim	Enable ethical conduct and moral reasoning	Prevent and combat unethical conduct and integrity violations
Behavioural assumptions	Social beings guided by values, principles, (public service) motivation and leaders and peers	Autonomous beings guided by economic self-interest
Policy	**Integrity approach**	**Compliance approach**
Methods and instruments	Internal controls, ethics education and training, communication and deliberation, ethical leadership, ethical culture and climate, reinforcement by rewards	External controls, education of rules and codes of conduct, reduced discretion and autonomy, auditing, monitoring and controls, reinforcement by sanctions
Implementation	**Integrity approach**	**Compliance approach**
Standards	Organizational mission, values and aspirations, social obligations, including law, rules, codes and norms	Criminal and regulatory law
Leadership and staffing	Managers, ethics officers	Lawyers, compliance officers
Activities	Lead (bottom-up) development of organizational values and standards, training and communication, integration in organizational system and culture, providing guidance and consultation, assessing values and performance, identifying and resolving problems and dilemmas	Developing (top-down) compliance standards, education and communication, handling reports of misconduct, conducting investigations, overseeing compliance audits and monitoring, enforcing standards with clear sanctions
Education and training	Ethical decision-making and values, dilemma training	Compliance standards and system, codes of conduct

Source: based on Paine (1994: 113)

EXERCISE 7.1 THE JOB DILEMMA

Imagine the following situation. You just graduated and have found a job at a dynamic, young and innovative company with many young people. Coincidentally, a good friend of your older brother is manager at the same department where you recently started working. His managing style, principles, values and expectations completely typify an integrity approach since he puts a lot of trust in your commitment and honesty as well as in that of your direct colleagues, without a set of many strict rules, and because you have relatively more freedom in terms of time management, working hours and the realization of tasks. Although you really like the working atmosphere, the company and the services they offer, your colleagues and manager, you unfortunately consider your job as very boring and you would rather want to put your efforts into something more challenging. Because of the good atmosphere, colleagues and good salary, you do not want to quit your job. Therefore, to still find the challenge that you miss in your job, you decide to start your own small business during the evening hours at home. With this brand new business plan of yours, you want to offer the same services as the company you work for on payroll basis, because you have a lot of affinity with this branch and you think you have a brilliant and innovative strategy. The crucial dilemma that you face, however, is that the realization of this plan would infringe upon the legally binding non-competition covenant that is integrated in the contract you have. Moreover, you also feel uncomfortable with the idea of putting the good relationship you have with your manager, who is also a friend of your brother, at risk, and to disadvantage the company you work on the basis of good labour conditions.

■ How would you resolve this ethical dilemma and what would be your course of action?

■ How would the integrity approach that your manager upholds influence your way of thinking about this dilemma and your decision to be made? Explain your decision.

■ What would your decision be in case your manager would steer business along the lines of the compliance approach? Explain your decision.

Commentary

In answering these complex questions, focus on the essentials of both the compliance approach and the integrity approach. These are, generally said, based on following rules, and following your own assessment of a situation, respectively. One could also consider the first approach as externally prescribed behaviour and the latter as intrinsically steered behaviour. Once again, however, one should bear in mind that the two approaches are not necessarily mutually exclusive and hence they can, and ideally should, complement each other. For example, Paine (1994) states that many integrity initiatives have structural features common to compliance-based initiatives such as a code of conduct and trainings in relevant areas of law.

Indeed, Lewis and Gilman (2005) argue for a 'fusion road' where the high road of integrity meets the low road of compliance. This is the route advocated by the OECD who similarly argue for a balanced approach (Global Forum on Public Governance 2009). This approach is based upon the challenges involved in implementing an integrity framework and they focus on aspects of organizational fairness rather than individual action. Thus, their framework includes guidance on structures, on personnel management, and on institutionalizing ethics.

EDUCATION AND TRAINING FOR ETHICAL DECISION-MAKING

Exercise 7.1 illustrates the importance of ethical decision-making. Regardless of the chosen ethics approach, ethics within organizations remains a matter of individual responsibility. Public officials working in and on behalf of the organization make the actual decisions and act upon them. In this respect Cooper (2006) speaks about the responsible administrator, who is bound to both objective and subjective responsibilities. Public officials have an objective responsibility in meeting the external expectations based on the law, organizational demands and societal values and norms. Thus, they are accountable for their ethical behaviour and actions, and moreover, have an obligation to fulfil certain tasks and to accomplish organizational and societal goals, including ethical obligations. However, public officials also have their own sense of duty. In this subjective responsibility, one's own moral compass is an important guide to ethical decisions and behaviour.

From our previous outline (see Table 7.1) it follows that a compliance approach will stress the importance of objective responsibilities, whereas an integrity approach will stress the significance of subjective responsibilities in ethical decision-making by public officials. These will subsequently become emphasized within organizational education and training programmes, which can, in turn, support the individual ethical decision-making of employees (cf. Lewis 1991).

In general, education and training refer to processes and experiences that are designed to impart knowledge, understanding and skills. More specifically, ethics education and training often offer cognitive programmes in ethical decision-making.

Underlying theoretical foundations generally assume that ethical decision-making involves four sequential sub-processes (cf. Butterfield, Treviño and Weaver 2000; Rest *et al.* 1999):

— **Moral sensitivity or awareness**: the recognition of the moral nature of a situation.
— **Moral judgement**: the decision of what is morally right in a situation.
— **Moral motivation or intent**: the decision to commit oneself to moral, rather than any other type of actions.
— **Moral character**: the demonstration and persistence to follow through on the intention to behave morally.

The aim and focus of ethics education and training is to prevent unethical conduct by raising individual moral awareness and improve moral judgement (either on the basis of compliance or self-governance), because these serve as an internal psychological guideline or condition for actual ethical behaviour (Treviño 1986). Or in other words, it is assumed that '[h]ow people think is related to what they do' (Treviño 1992: 446; cf. Blasi 1980; Lasthuizen 2008).

Furthermore, it is supposed that an individual's level of cognitive moral development strongly influences moral judgement (Treviño 1986, 1992). We might also consider self-regulation and reflection, and the development of this from a psychological perspective (Bandura 1991). Indeed, the cognitive moral development theory developed by Kohlberg (1969), which remains a leading and widely applied theory and is discussed in Chapter 2 (e.g. Rest *et al.* 1999), does not focus on the ethical decision itself but on how individuals decide on what is right. The basic model used to assess such a development consists of six stages that can be understood in terms of three broad levels: preconventional (the lowest level); conventional; and principled (the highest level):

— **Preconventional** individuals are primarily concerned with their own interests; what is good, is what is good for them. Thus, they seek to avoid punishment by the 'authorities', the significant others that set the rules. Pre-conventional individuals therefore weigh the interests of others against their own benefits in a sort of 'tit for tat' strategy (Axelrod 1984).
— **Conventional** individuals conform to the expectations of the significant others that form their group; good is that which is in accordance with the group norm or rule.
— **Principled** individuals are guided by the principles of justice and (human) rights (see Chapter 2) and make decisions on the basis of self-chosen ethical principles (Treviño 1986); i.e. their own intrinsic moral compass (Denkers, in van Beers 2001).

Moral development research among adults and within different professions (e.g. Rest *et al.* 1999; Rest and Narvaez 1994) suggests that the large majority of adults reason at the conventional level of cognitive moral development. In other words, most employees can be typified as conventional individuals who look outside themselves for guidance by rules and laws, and follow the perceived expectations of significant others within their (direct) environments (Treviño and Brown 2005). Accordingly, it is plausible to believe that organizations can raise moral awareness and moral judgement; for example by offering ethics education and training programmes. Additionally, because leaders, and especially immediate supervisors, play an authority role (and are therefore likely to be significant others for employees), they should be a key source of moral guidance, a point we return to in Chapter 9. By acting as such, they offer further opportunities for the organization to influence employees' moral awareness and moral judgement, which are also greatly affected by the organization's ethical culture (see Chapter 5).

Most training programmes in cognitive moral reasoning are offering a practical ethical decision-making model. One such widely used and applied model was developed by Cooper (2006). We will describe this model in Figure 7.1, but first some final remarks about the effectiveness of education and training programmes.

In practice, another common goal of ethics education and training is providing employees with the 'right' ethical framework. As discussed previously, such a compliance strategy to organizational ethics seems less successful. In part this is related to the ethics orientation of compliance strategies. In the literature there is growing consensus that the emphasis should be put on the identification and application of one's own sets of values, because of their basic impact on moral judgements (Falkenberg and Woiceshyn 2008). Another factor that enhances the effect of ethics education and training is a design in reference to the target group, which means that characteristics such as age, level of education, work experience and work features, like the position and the level of autonomy, have to be taken into account. Furthermore, Thorne LeClair and Ferrel (2000) state that training professionals on a sensitive subject requires that training meets the following critical elements.

- The training situation should parallel the work situation or decision environment, for which using ethics cases, real-life situations and work-related ethical dilemmas are essential (cf. Falkenberg and Woiceshyn 2008; Weber 2007).
- Stimulus variation and interactive learning.
- Presentation of the rules of the training condition.
- Conditions of the learning environment, especially safety and the trainer's trustworthiness and facilitation.

Box 7.2 summarizes four useful and essential moments in professional life.

BOX 7.2 ETHICS LEARNING MOMENTS IN THE PROFESSIONAL CAREER

Although ethics training is relevant to all employees, four specific moments in a person's organizational career are seen as most important to advance and maintain professional ethical acting (cf. Huberts, forthcoming):

1. To become aware of the ethics aspects of professional life and understand the meaning of the guiding organizational values and principles in daily practice, public officials should be best educated and trained **right from the start** in the organization.
2. To reflect on specific work-related dilemmas and to confront objective with subjective responsibilities, and formal with informal practices, public officials should be educated and trained **shortly after the start** in their working environment.
3. To become aware and discuss the specific ethics issues, aspects and risks of their position, public officials should be educated and trained **when moving to a new ethically vulnerable position.**
4. To become ethically competent as a leader and be able to realize ethical leadership, public officials should be educated and trained in special leadership programmes, **when moving to a leadership position.**

AN ETHICAL DECISION-MAKING MODEL

To practise and learn how to deal with ethical issues and dilemmas that public officials are confronted with on a daily basis, Cooper (2006) suggests using a practical decision-making framework or model for systematic reflection. This can be used by individuals or groups to analyze and resolve such problems within the context of the public organization. As Cooper (2006: 18) states,

> ethical issues arise in many forms for administrators, but they nearly always raise difficult questions of administrative responsibility.

We mostly address ethical problems not at the level of thorough ethical analysis, but instead we react and judge spontaneously based on our feelings and emotions, or from the level of moral rules that seem important to us, such as personal or social values, religion or professional rules and codes. Usually this will do; we reach a decision by applying our available repertoire of practical moral rules (Cooper 2006).

However, when these available moral trade-offs do not work or evoke tensions, a more systematic reflection on the underlying ethical principles might be necessary

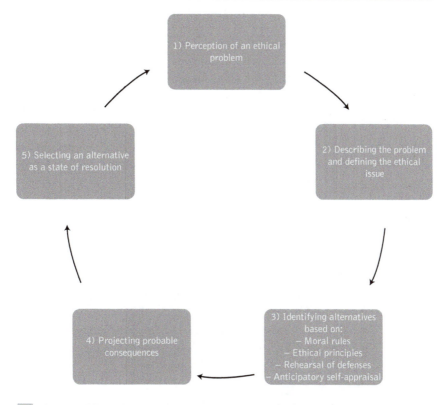

Figure 7.1 *Ethical decision-making in five steps*

Source: based on the Ethical Decision-Making Model by Cooper (2006: 31)

to come to a decision on the ethical issue at hand. Even in less complex cases, applying a more structured approach could result in more self-awareness, clarity and conscious choices about our course of action and its basis. Thus, by using an ethical decision-making model, such as shown in Figure 7.1, the skills for thinking in a more principled fashion can be developed.

THE FIVE STEPS

1. Perception of an ethical problem

In daily situations we do not always recognize the ethical dimensions and implications of the problems we face. Nevertheless, in many professional decision-making situations ethics does play a role and public officials are confronted with conflicts between values that are equally important (cf. Geuras and Garofalo 2005). The first step is to become aware of this gap and map the ethical problem.

2. Describing the problem and defining the ethical issue

The second step is to objectively describe the facts of the situation: who are the actors and stakeholders that are involved, what are their viewpoints, the events and issues, and what are the ethical risks and challenges? What do we know and what information is still missing? Which standpoints should we question from an ethics perspective? From the answers to the following questions the ethical issue at stake can be defined. Which ethical values and principles, loyalties, responsibilities and/or obligations conflict or compete in the situation of decision-making and which show overlap or similarities? Which values and principles cause the biggest ethical problem in the practical dilemma?

3. Identifying alternatives

The third step is to identify all alternative courses of action. What are the options? What are the consequences and implications of each option, what are the pros and cons? For instance, do the alternatives fit with the moral rules and ethical principles? (See Chapter 2.) And, what about your own values and norms, and those of the wider audience? So, what are the creative solutions for the problem?

It is crucial in this phase to avoid thinking in 'black or white' terms; all possible solutions should be equally discussed vis-à-vis their merits: '[t]his either-or view is the most common trap in the ethical process' (Cooper 2006: 34).

4. Projecting probable consequences

Projecting the positive and negative anticipated consequences of alternatives is the fourth step. Use your moral imagination to construct a scenario with actors, interaction and implications for each alternative. Connect rational aspects (coherency, plausibility of the alternatives) and affective aspects (accompanying feelings) of the ethical decision-making.

5. Selecting an alternative as a state of resolution

You can subsequently make a decision and choose the 'best' course of action. Be sure that the decision is in line with your own personal values and moral compass, and that it would be accepted by the wider environment by taking 'the newspaper test': can you still defend your choice when you are on the front page of tomorrow's newspaper? If so, we have found a fit:

> Resolution is reached when we discover an alternative that provides an acceptable balance of our duty to principle and the likely consequences and satisfies our need to have sound reasons for our conduct and our need to be satisfied with the decision.

> (Cooper 2006: 38)

EXERCISE 7.2   THE HOLIDAY DILEMMA

Mr Brown is the head of IT in the public sector, for a large municipality which has been subject to recent public management reforms in terms of increasing commercialization. For his work, he has been invited by a large IT company to present at a conference in southern France. Because the municipality he works for uses a lot of their software, he has been able to build up a number of good relationships with people in the company.

In addition to his travel and accommodation expenses the company is willing to pay for his partner to come as well. As the conference takes place during the summer, it seems like a good idea to Mr Brown to integrate his holiday in this work visit. This way, he argues, he will be able to go on holiday for next to nothing.

Before concluding this chapter, we suggest you practise with the ethical decision-making model by means of Exercise 7.2. Please read the ethical dilemma carefully, follow the steps in the model (see Figure 7.1) and answer the discussion questions before coming to a final decision.

Discussion questions

- What is/are the key ethical issue(s) underlying the situation?
- Who are involved, which stakeholders?
- Identify the possible intended and unintended consequences of this issue or these issues.
- In case of multiple issues, which one is more unethical and why?
- What universal principles that are subject to the public sector are directly related to the situation and in what ways are they put at risk? See for an overview Box 1.1 and Table 6.3.
- In what ways could an integrity-based approach encourage Mr Brown to make the 'right' decision in terms of ethical and legitimate behaviour?
- How would a compliance-based approach differ from an integrity approach in this regard, and in what ways would it result in a more effective or less effective outcome?
- As a consultant, advise Mr Brown in how to deal with this situation and which decision to make. In formulating the advice, also include the arguments that support the decision that ought to be taken. Use the 'steps model' (Figure 7.1) to come to a decision.

129

Commentary

In deliberating the situation, one should bear in mind the following. First, the nature and raison d'être of both the public and private sector often differ considerably. Certain principles that are inherent to the public sector are incompatible with private sector principles and vice versa. In thinking about possible consequences of the identified issues, one should focus on the extent of incompatibility of these different principles.

Second, although in an ideal world one would assume that organizational culture leads and influences individual behaviour according to predefined principles and values, both individuals employed in the public and private sector infringe rules or act contrarily to important values. Next to the individual level, one should also doubt the homogeneity of the organizational culture itself and recognize also that public sector organizations are dynamic and subject to sub-cultures and competing values.

Third, think about the information you need in order to formulate appropriate advice.

In sum, one should take into account various levels and types of governance that affect the outcome of individual behaviour, like the type of sector, departmental norms, professional and organizational values and individual perspectives. In addition, one should be aware of the information one needs in order to formulate advice for taking a suitable decision.

CONCLUSIONS

One key question is what can the organization do to facilitate ethical behaviour? One, under-researched, response is how organizations might recognize the value of dissent in organizations and create channels through which that dissent might be expressed (O'Leary 2006). This is not just introducing whistle-blowing procedures, but how an organization can learn from dissenting opinions, thus avoiding the dangers of 'group think' where accepted norms and conventions get in the way of critical thinking. It does take courage to stand against accepted organizational wisdom, and a key role of managers is to support staff who wish to disagree, provided of course that such dissent is driven by organizational and public interests and not by personal interests.

This chapter has focused on the integrity approach to organizational ethics, thereby describing its orientation, policies and instruments. Moreover, it clarified the way of implementing this approach within an organization. Furthermore, we discussed the differences between this strategy and the compliance approach in Chapter 6. Central to ethics education and training programmes, which are embedded in an integrity approach, are cognitive programmes in ethical decision-making. We have described an ethical decision-making model that enables you to solve ethical dilemmas and arrive at a sound decision that corresponds to the role of a responsible administrator.

REFERENCES

Axelrod, R. (1984) *The Evolution of Cooperation*. New York: Basic Books.

Bandura, A. (1991) 'Social Cognitive Theory of Self-regulation', *Organizational Behavior and Human Decision Processes* 50 (2): 248–87.

Beers, P. van (ed.) (2001) *Frans Denkers' moreel kompas van de politie* [Frans Denkers' moral compass of the police] Den Hong: Politia Nova.

Blasi, A. (1980) 'Bridging Moral Cognition and Moral Action: A Critical Review of the Literature', *Psychological Bulletin* 88 (1): 1–45.

Butterfield, K., Treviño, L.K. and Weaver, G.R. (2000) 'Moral Awareness in Business Organizations: Influences of Issue-related and Social Context Factors', *Human Relations* 53 (7): 981–1018.

Cooper, T.L. (2006) *The Responsible Administrator: An Approach to Ethics for the Administrative Role*. 5th edition. San Francisco, CA: Jossey-Bass. [Originally published 1998.]

Falkenberg, L. and Woiceshyn, J. (2008) 'Enhancing Business Ethics: Using Cases to Teach Moral Reasoning', *Journal of Business Ethics* 79 (3): 213–17.

Geuras, D. and Garofalo, C. (2005) *Practical Ethics in Public Administration*. 2nd edition. Vienna, VA: Management Concepts.

Global Forum on Public Governance (2009) 'Towards a Sound Integrity Framework: Instruments, Processes, Structures and Conditions for Implementation', GOV/PGC/GF(2009)1. Paris: OECD.

Gong, T. (2011) 'An "Institutional Turn" in Integrity Management in China', *International Review of Administrative Sciences* 77 (4): 671–86.

Jaques, E. (1990) 'In Praise of Hierarchy', *Harvard Business Review* 68 (1): 127–33.

Huberts, L.W.J.C. (forthcoming). *Integrity of Governance: Perspectives in Research and Policies on Ethics, Integrity and Integritism*.

Kohlberg, L. (1969) 'State and Sequence: The Cognitive-development Approach to Socialization' in Goslin, D.A. (ed.) *Handbook of Socialization Theory and Research*. Chicago, IL: Rand McNally, pp. 347–480.

Lasthuizen, K.M. (2008) *Leading to Integrity: Empirical Research into the Effects of Leadership on Ethics and Integrity*. Enschede, the Netherlands: Printpartners Ipskamp.

Lewis, C.W. (1991) *The Ethics Challenge in Public Service: A Problem Solving Guide*. San Francisco, CA: Jossey-Bass.

Lewis, C.W. and Gilman, S.C. (2005) *The Ethics Challenge in Public Service: A Problem-solving Guide*. 2nd edition. San Francisco, CA: Jossey-Bass.

O'Leary, R. (2006) 'The Ethics of Dissent: Managing Guerrilla Government', *Public Integrity* 9 (1): 97–109.

Paine, L.S. (1994) 'Managing for Organizational Integrity', *Harvard Business Review* 72 (2):106–17.

Rest, J.R. and Narvaez, D. (eds) (1994) *Moral Development in the Professions*. Hillsdale, NJ: Lawrence Erlbaum.

Rest, J.R., Narvaez, D., Bebeau, M.J. and Thoma, S.J. (1999) *Postconventional Moral Thinking: A Neo-Kohlbergian Approach*. Mahwah, NJ: Lawrence Erlbaum.

Rohr, J.A. (1989) *Ethics for Bureaucrats: An Essay on Law and Value*. 2nd edition. New York: Marcel Decker, Inc.

Thorne LeClair, D.T. and Ferrell, L. (2000) 'Innovation in Experiential Business Ethics Training', *Journal of Business Ethics* 23 (3): 313–22.

Treviño, L.K. (1986) 'Ethical Decision Making in Organizations: A Person-Situation Interactionist Model', *Academy of Management Review* 11 (3): 601–17.

—— (1992) 'Moral Reasoning and Business Ethics: Implications for Research, Education and Management', *Journal of Business Ethics* 11 (5,6): 445–59.

Treviño, L.K. and Brown, M.E. (2005) 'The Role of Leaders in Influencing Unethical Behavior in the Workplace' in Kidwell, R.E. Jr. and Martin, C.L. (eds) *Managing Organizational Deviance*. Thousand Oaks, CA, London and New Delhi: Sage Publications, pp. 69–96.

Treviño L.K., Weaver, G.R., Gibson, D.G. and Toffler, B.L. (1999) 'Managing Ethics and Legal Compliance: What Works and What Hurts?' *California Management Review* 41 (2): 131–51.

Weber, J.A. (2007) 'Business Ethics Training: Insights from Learning Theory', *Journal of Business Ethics* 70 (1): 61–85.

Chapter 8

Ethical performance

How do we know if we are doing the right thing and can we improve?

LEARNING OBJECTIVES

By the end of this chapter you should:

- understand the concept of ethical performance
- be able to analyze the different dimensions of an ethical performance framework
- understand some of the philosophical, technical and implementation issues associated with ethical performance
- be able to illustrate how public sector organizations have measured ethical performance.

KEY POINTS IN THIS CHAPTER

- Drivers of performance improvement are many, complex, interrelated and sometimes difficult to measure.
- Trends show a growth in performance, audit and inspection regimes for public agencies and attempts to measure ethical performance.
- Different stakeholders have different expectations of performance and it is difficult to capture all of these stakeholder interests in one performance regime.
- Ethical issues in public service organizations are a mixture of individual motivations, organizational imperatives and societal values.
- Trends in ethical frameworks have moved from relying on personal integrity to compliance systems of control.

- We do not have enough research evidence to argue that ethical leadership, a code of conduct, or training will have the greatest impact, and we also do not know the impact of external regulation and inspection.
- Ethical audit has to reflect both individual performance and organizational setting and should consist of a number of different parts.

KEY TERMS

- **Ethical framework** – part of the overall approach to governance issues with an emphasis on prevention rather than cure or punishment.
- **Ethical performance** – how well individuals and organizations perform from an ethical point of view.
- **Ethical impact** – the difference that ethical performance can make to key stakeholders.

INTRODUCTION

Much of the public services are dominated by performance measurement and management regimes and the development of key performance indicators. Public officials have been subject to performance regimes both as part of their own development, and also as part of organizational-wide regimes expected to demonstrate efficiency, effectiveness, responsiveness and so on. Such developments are all part of the drive for accountability for the spending of taxpayers' money. The drivers of performance improvement are many and complex and it is not always clear what impact individual drivers, or the combination of different drivers, have on performance outcomes (see Ashworth, Boyne and Entwistle 2010). Given the increase in the number of measures to ensure ethical behaviour and curb unethical behaviour (documented in Chapters 6 and 7), it is appropriate to ask if any of these measures have been successful. And yet, the concept of organizational ethical performance is a rather puzzling one; in what sense can the ethical health of an organization be measured? Indeed, how can we define the ethical organization? Is it the sum of the quality of individual acts carried out by an organization's members, the existence of an ethical culture, howsoever defined, or the extent to which an organization fulfils its social and community obligations? These are not abstract questions. Increasingly organizations are being assessed against some measure of ethical performance. This raises a host of issues and in this chapter we explore the philosophical, technical and implementation issues associated with the notion of ethical performance, all of which are interlinked. We see all three as important components in the development of an ethical framework, and form three points of a triangle as depicted in Figure 8.1.

Philosophical issues

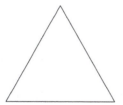

Technical issues   **Implementation issues**

Figure 8.1 Organizational ethics performance framework

The philosophical issues relate to the understanding of moral agency and include the ethical health of an organization, the notion of ethical performance, and the ascription of responsibility and the problem of many hands (Thompson 1980). As public services are delivered through teams and increasingly through a multitude of different agencies, where do we ascribe responsibility? The technical issues relate to the development of a set of indicators that measure ethical performance, and the possibility of setting an ethical benchmark. The implementation issues concern the importance of ethical leadership, top-down versus bottom-up approaches to policy implementation and the challenges in embedding an ethical culture throughout the organization.

Many of these issues are not specific to ethical performance but are relevant for performance measurement and management generally. All are interrelated and pose different types of questions. The questions are both normative and practical. The most difficult ones to address are the philosophical ones; at the same time, the technical issues are problematic insofar as they are related to the philosophical ones.

Attempts at measuring ethical performance are growing in number. This chapter describes the background to this development, addresses a number of conceptual issues concerned with it, outlines attempts to develop tools to measure it, and explores how individual public agencies are furthering this development.

BACKGROUND

Recent years have seen a growth in performance, audit and inspection regimes for public agencies. Ethics has not been immune from such growth; in central and local government in the UK and elsewhere, ethical frameworks have been introduced to govern the behaviour of both elected and appointed public officials. The UK for example, has witnessed a move from a reliance on personal integrity to a compliance system of control. The OECD has a long-standing interest in the effectiveness of integrity measures and argues for a combination of a values-based approach and a rules-based approach (OECD 2005, 2009).

Despite the introduction of ethical frameworks, it is not obvious that ethical performance has improved (assuming of course that it is possible to measure ethical performance), nor that, for example, trust in politicians has grown. Indeed, the creation of anti-corruption agencies to oversee ethical frameworks often has the perverse effect of increasing the number of complaints concerning unethical conduct. The creation of such an agency often provides a vehicle for complaints that did not exist before. We discuss this below.

However, the impetus behind a concern with ethical performance can be located in several areas: first, the growth in regulation and the audit explosion (Hood *et al.* 1998); second, in the concern of organizations such as the EU that membership to the EU from the transitional States is dependent upon their demonstrating that they are putting in place measures to combat corruption and that these will be effective; third, a concern on the part of international agencies, such as the UN, that any aid cannot just disappear into the Swiss bank accounts of the leaders of those countries that are the recipients of aid.

Yet, the ethical environment of an organization is complex and strategies to develop such an environment have changed over time. Historically, at least in the public sector, organizations focused upon detection and punishment of corruption, fraud and bribery. These concerns were the driving force behind the creation of such agencies as Transparency International (TI) and the Australian and Hong Kong Independent Commissions Against Corruption (ICAC). More recently, interest has concentrated on preventive measures through ethical awareness training and civic education. This is often associated with codes of conduct, which can have an aspirational and guiding role as well as a regulatory function. Currently there is considerable interest in ethical review and audit, and assessing the performance of interventions designed to strengthen ethical standing.

Increasingly, then, ethical issues that face organizations are recognized to be much wider in scope than misconduct, fraud, corruption and bribery. Indeed, the Seven Principles of Public Life, introduced in the UK in response to corrupt behaviour on the part of members of parliament, and discussed in Chapter 6, are concerned with promoting standards of good conduct as much as identifying illegal or unethical behaviour. It is recognized that the less obvious ethical issues such as respect for persons, civility and standards of common decency are just as important as identifying examples of illegal or improper behaviour and punishing it. Of course, the latter are more easily recognized and definable in performance measurement terms.

THE NATURE OF PERFORMANCE

Organizations, and individuals, need to be clear about what they are supposed to be doing and how they are to be held to account for what they do. It is particularly important for public service organizations and public officials as they are spending taxpayers' money. Yet the goals of public sector organizations are not always clear and are often ambiguous or, indeed, may be in conflict. A performance system may have multiple purposes and meet the needs of different stakeholders. For example, Behn (2003) identifies a number of functions for the performance of public service organizations:

– **Evaluation**: focuses on how well the organization is performing.
– **Control**: concerned with ensuring that staff are doing the right thing.
– **Motivation** of staff to do what is necessary to, for example, improve integrity and fight corruption.
– **Promotion**: convincing political superiors, legislators, stakeholders, journalists and citizens that the organization is doing a good job.
– **Celebration** of success – an important organizational ritual.
– **Learning** which focuses on policies or practices that are working or not working.
– **Improvement**: concerned with acting to improve performance.

Each of these, however, raise interesting issues from the perspective of ethical performance. Thus, in evaluating the organization do we focus on its ability to raise resources (inputs); its activities in terms of the speed at which it, for example, processes complaints (throughputs); the reduction in the number of, for example, corruption cases (outputs); or the increase in trust in public officials (outcomes)? There is also a theoretical framework of legitimacy that also distinguishes between 'input' legitimacy, 'throughput' legitimacy and 'output' legitimacy (see, e.g. Bekkers *et al.* 2007; Keohane and Nye 2001; Scharpf 1999). We also might want to think about the ways in which different stakeholders have different expectations of performance. Citizens will want their public officials to use public funds honestly and to the advantage of the majority; politicians may be concerned with performance that enhances their chances of winning the next election; agency chiefs might be interested in the efficiency of the organization; professional staff may focus on doing their best for their patients or clients irrespective of cost. It is difficult to capture all of these stakeholder interests in one performance regime.

One feature of performance that has dominated has been the use of performance for judgement as expressed in, for example, league tables. Thus we have a league table of the most corrupt regimes, the Transparency International Corruption Perception Index, which includes a league table of countries perceived to be corrupt, and can be used to beat poorly performing countries around the head. A different approach sees performance in terms of learning and development, focusing on improvement. Of course the notion of ethical improvement is a tricky one; not only that but the relationship between cause and effect is rarely clear. We do not have a theory of ethical impact which demonstrates that, for example, ethical leadership or the creation of an anti-corruption agency or a code of conduct is directly responsible for this or that change in ethical behaviour.

PHILOSOPHICAL ISSUES

There are a number of fundamental issues that need to be considered, focusing upon the nature of moral agency, the organizational context of individual agency and the ethical status of an organization as an entity in itself.

In the first instance, the position we take will depend upon our view of moral agency. Thus, Bauman (1993) for example, contends that ethics cannot be located within organizational life. He sees ethical phenomena as inherently non-rational, insofar as they precede the considerations of purpose and the calculation of means–ends. Thus, according to this view, there is no role for ethics in purposive organizations:

> Reason cannot help the moral self without depriving the self of what makes the self moral: that unfounded, non-rational, un-arguable, no excuses given and non-calculable urge to stretch towards the other, to caress, to be for, to live for, happen what may. Reason is about making correct decisions, while moral responsibility precedes all thinking about decisions as it does not, and cannot care about any logic which would allow the approval of an action as correct.
>
> (Bauman 1993: 247)

It is, therefore, inappropriate to assess any ethical action against some notion of correct or incorrect behaviour or ethical performance. The post-modern theme is pursued by Charles Taylor (1991), who identifies the 'malaise' of modern life, due to, firstly, individualism; secondly, the primacy of instrumental reason; and thirdly, the institutions and structures of industrial and technological society that severely restrict our choices. According to Taylor, the first is about the loss of meaning in our lives, the second is about the eclipse of ends and the third is about the loss of freedom.

Authenticity is about 'being true to oneself' but, for Taylor, this need not necessarily mean egotism or atomism, since being true to oneself takes place against a backcloth of social and economic history that gives it meaning! We need relationships, at least to fulfil ourselves even if no longer to define us. We find our identities only against a background of things that matter. Taylor contends that the manner of our orientation is self-referential but the content may be something beyond ourselves. We find fulfilment in our relationships with others as, say, a parent or a friend and we need to enter into dialogue with others.

The relationship with others is particularly significant for public officials:

> it is in small individual acts expressed through a set of relationships that the public service ethos comes to light. The manager gives expression to the ethos through dealing with people in terms of care, diligence, courtesy and integrity. The public service ethos is best perceived through the quality of these face-to-face relationships, through processes as much as results.
>
> (Lawton 1998: 69)

Uhr (1999) suggests that the issue is further complicated for public servants who, by definition, take on certain responsibilities and duties arising from their office. He argues that the obligations of role give rise to two levels of public service responsibility as an:

— agent of the public with duties and obligations towards the public
— agency employee with duties and obligations flowing from the specific mission of the agency in question.

However, this view assumes that there is agreement in organization values and clarity of duties and responsibilities. It is not always obvious that agreed-upon values are adopted in practice.

A number of positions can be taken regarding the moral nature of individuals within organizations, reflecting different views on the relationships between individuals within it and with the organization as a whole. The first view sees individuals as morally neutral, allowing the organization to imprint its own goals, targets and values on the individual. It is in this sense that as we discussed in Chapter 4, culture can be managed. The ends of the organization are of supreme importance and were we to judge its performance ethically we might wish to call upon some version of utilitarianism. The classical version of public administration accords with the morally neutral bureaucrat implementing policy formulated by others, and judged upon its effectiveness or impact. In contrast to this view, as long as officials have discretion and choice they cannot escape from making moral decisions.

A second view might see organizations not just as purposive enterprises but as co-operative enterprises where individuals are recognized as the organization's greatest asset. In reality we know that managers manipulate others and are, in turn, themselves manipulated. However, we do have expectations of our public officials and we require them to always act out of a sense of duty, acting to further the public interest.

Organizations themselves will also have rules, both formal and informal, that circumscribe the actions of individuals. Some of these rules will demand ethical behaviour, others will be neutral. At the same time, public service organizations, in particular, are expected to respond to the interests of citizens, clients and customers and some of these expectations will be concerned with the standards of conduct of both elected and appointed officials.

What impacts the role and duty of public servants is the organizational context and the demands made upon individuals by those organizations. Whether an organization itself can have a conscience and can be ascribed moral responsibility is a moot point. Maclagan (1998) takes the view that it is ultimately down to individual responsibility. At the same time, Di Maggio and Powell (1991) identify the need for public organizations to conform to external values in their environment through isomorphism and it may well be that judgements about right and wrong are as much community decisions as individual ones. Thus, ethical issues in public service organizations are a mixture of individual motivations, organizational imperatives and societal values (see Lawton 2005).

TECHNICAL ISSUES

Just as challenging as philosophical issues are the technical issues associated with performance. Notwithstanding the complexity of performance measurement and management in the public sector (Noordegraaf and Abma 2003), the key technical questions are: which indicators are appropriate? Should they be aimed at the individual, teams or the organization as a whole, and how do we ascribe responsibility? At the same time, we need to pay respect to the usual criteria associated with performance indicators such as timeliness, validity, reliability, relevance, specificity and so on (see Holloway 1999). We also need to consider how the indicators reflect the stated values of the organization, particularly those rather abstract values associated with the public service ethos. For example, should our criteria be built around the Principles of Public Life, initially established by the Nolan Committee? Agreement in values is important here. Whatever performance indicators are used they will have to meet a number of criteria:

- Be clear and unambiguous, and readily understandable.
- Be relevant; they must reveal something of interest.
- Satisfy validity; do the indicators measure what we want to measure?
- Be reliable, do they produce the same result when used by different people?
- Be acceptable politically; but at the same time recognize that there may be certain classes of action that should not be compromised.
- Cannot be manipulated to serve vested interests or to distort results.
- Be reasonably cheap to collect.

- Be coherent and fit into a wider whole, particularly the philosophy, culture, values and goals of the wider organization.
- Timeliness insofar as there is an awareness of how long it takes for the effect of, for example, a new code of conduct, to become evident. Can it capture both short-term and long-term effects?
- Ensure accuracy by taking care when recording data.
- Consider feasibility and realistic expectations.
- Be sensitive to detect the levels of change that we want to observe.
- Apply to all levels within an organization.
- Be sensitive to the different functions, and demands upon, different parts of the organization.

Our first concern is with what are we measuring: is it processes or outcomes, is it individuals or organizations? Where performance indicators (PI) are designed only to look at outcomes, then deontological explanations that focus on the means not the ends may not be appropriate. Where we are concerned with processes rather than ends then, in the context of the public services where it is a moot point that the process or the service is the outcome and where the way you treat people matters, a Kantian perspective will be appropriate. We might also have to say something about the nature of ethical standards such as, what are we measuring against? Are there universal values? What is the ethical equivalent of the generally accepted accounting principles (GAAP) that accountants and auditors subscribe to (see Satava, Caldwell and Richards 2006)?

Presumably we can only measure what people do, not what they say they would do as reported in, for example, a survey. We cannot measure their intentions. This point is of particular relevance given that unethical outcomes often result from lack of knowledge or incompetence rather than evil intent. Similarly, is a concern with ethical standards linked to strategy as part of what the organization stands for or are they tagged on and seen as getting in the way of more important financial considerations? (Many organizations might argue that they cannot afford to be ethical but there is evidence to suggest that ethical concerns are increasingly taken into account in terms of reputation, which does feed into the bottom line for private sector organizations.)

Putting aside these considerations for the moment, we can envisage the kinds of questions that ethical PIs might explore, including:

- Does the act cause more harm than good? We might use some form of cost-benefit analysis here.
- Were rights protected and obligations fulfilled?
- Was accountability assured?
- Was justice done?
- Were freedoms protected?

- Was consent given?
- Was individual autonomy protected?
- Was quality maintained?
- Was waste avoided?
- Was effective use made of public funds?
- Were professional standards complied with?
- Were organizational standards complied with?

EXERCISE 8.1 LONDON BOROUGH PERFORMANCE INDICATORS (PIS)

This authority has used a number of indicators to assess the health of the authority in relation to standards and ethics and they are tracked every quarter. They include:

- District Audit Public Interest reports
- Objections to the council's accounts
- Referrals to, and investigations undertaken by, the Standards Board for England
- Number of whistle-blowing incidents
- Number of challenges to procurement decisions
- Disciplinary action relating to breaches of the Member/Officer protocol
- Disciplinary action relating to fraud
- Freedom of Information issues
- Industrial action
- Number of employment tribunals
- Number of ombudsman complaints received and settled

Discussion

By using such a 'metrics' approach, performance can be tracked on a year-by-year basis and thus provide useful information. Of itself, however, can such indicators tell the whole story? What other data needs to support such metrics?

Many of the indicators can be measured objectively; others cannot and rely on perceptual surveys. Some might just result from good management. However, as well as explaining individual acts we might examine the organization in terms of: does it have a values statement; does it have a code of conduct; does it follow all the legal requirements; does it have an ethics training programme?

BOX 8.1   PERCEPTUAL SURVEY

Question: Why should I trust my boss? S/he:

	Always						Never
	1	2	3	4	5	6	7
Explains actions to me							
Listens to my point of view							
Encourages staff to work ethically							
Acts ethically							
Keeps commitments							
Does not take undue advantage							
Is open and transparent							
Puts staff interests first							
Discourages staff from bending the rules							

See ICAC (1998)

Given the importance of relationships that we identified above, then we also need to consider how to measure the relationships aspects. Were promises kept, was the contract fulfilled and was trust established? The latter can only be captured in a perceptual survey. Box 8.1 provides an example of what might be included in such a survey.

We return to trust and performance later in this chapter. As with any performance measurement system, there may be a tendency to evaluate that which is easily evaluated. For example, measure structures and procedures in terms of equal opportunities, health and safety at work legislation and so on. Such an approach will follow a 'low road' to ethics that concentrates upon compliance rather than governance in a wider sense and encourages a belief that if an act is not proscribed by law then it must be acceptable. Similarly, issues such as procedural fairness can be measured but other issues are more problematic. How do we measure whether respect for persons is given, for example?

The challenge is to turn abstract principles into concrete acts. Table 8.1 provides examples of what these might include.

Table 8.1 *Principles into practice*

Accountability	Breaking the rules
Transparency	Refusing to justify decisions
Honesty	Use of office equipment for personal use
Impartiality	Favouritism
Leadership	Treating junior staff badly
Confidentiality	Unauthorized disclosure to further private interests
Acting in the public interest	Putting private interests first
Responsiveness	Undue delay in dealing with the public
Legality	Abuse of power
Accessibility	Refusing to give out authorized information

If we take just one of the principles in Table 8.2 as an example, then we can see what high and low performance might include.

The unit of analysis is also important. Rarely is the solution to ethical issues found in one area – it might be a combination of internal organizational factors, such as a code of conduct, or external factors such as a vigilant media or an ombudsman. Public service organizations are part of a wider system in much the same way that an ethical framework will have to recognize the impact of institutions and actors at different levels. At national level the justice department, audit office, ombudsman or a national anti-corruption agency will all have a role to play in combating corruption. At municipal level, the media, local ombudsman, or a local

Table 8.2 *Does the leadership of the organization demonstrate and promote, through personal example, ethical standards?*

Focus	High performance	Low performance
Treatment of staff	Respect for views of staff Acts as a role model	Treats staff badly Does not defend staff Favours certain individuals
Respect for citizens	Open communication and co-operation Listens	Ignores their views and needs Does not provide a forum for discussion
Promote the public interest	Serves the common good	Seeks to make personal gain through public office Does not declare conflicts of interest
The vision/values of the organization	Has a clear vision of what an ethical organization looks like	Ethics are not part of the values of the organization

integrity agency might be involved. At agency level, a code of conduct, peer support, training or leadership will be important. At the moment we do not know enough about which of these factors (or more likely, a combination of factors), impacts ethical performance and what might moderate or mediate corruption the most.

IMPLEMENTATION ISSUES

At the risk of oversimplifying the vast body of work on policy implementation, it is clear that implementation is problematic. In many areas of public policy there is an implementation gap between the policy formulated and how it takes effect 'on the ground' (see Barrett 2004; Schofield 2004).

Quite clearly it is desirable to assess the extent to which, for our purposes, an ethical policy, delivered through an ethical framework, is successful or not. It is, however, a completely different matter for individual organizations to seek and develop an ethical culture, to change values and individual behaviours. This is an exercise of a completely different order, and it requires, as we argue below, different tools for implementation.

The problems with 'top-down' implementation are well known and are generally characterized as resulting either from a poorly formulated policy in the first place or, in the second place, the lack of capability or capacity of those charged with the responsibility for implementation. Thus, any organizational change has to be embedded within the organization as a whole and we know that this is not straightforward. There are a number of implementation issues identified in the literature including:

> The lack of time and insufficient resources. Generally, change is driven by the need to respond quickly to a set of changing circumstances and not enough time is available to think through and implement changes. For example, the introduction of anti-corruption measures often results from bad publicity concerning one or more scandals amongst politicians. Policy-makers have to be seen to respond quickly and are driven as much by the timing of the next election as by the detailed consideration of policy alternatives.
>
> Unforeseen problems. It is almost impossible to predict in advance all the possible problems and issues that may arise in advance of the implementation of a policy itself.
>
> The need for co-ordination amongst a multiplicity of actors. As public services are delivered, increasingly, by a range of different providers, it becomes more and more difficult to reconcile different values, goals and practices.
>
> The possibility of distractions. The electoral cycle engages the attentions of politicians more or less fully during different periods of the cycle.

145

The lack of skills. Policies are made without thinking through the requirements in terms of those who are charged with implementation.

Inadequate training, which can apply to behavioural skills as much as technical skills.

A hostile environment. Public services are delivered in a goldfish bowl as public scrutiny, including the media, demands transparency.

Lack of leadership. Without a policy champion the best-intended policies may sit on shelves gathering dust.

Lack of detail such that key implementation tasks may not have been clarified.

Lack of clear objectives, such that the intended goals are not clear and there is a mismatch between the intended objectives and the tools available to meet those objectives.

Lack of communication.

Tasks not specified in the correct sequence.

(See Rose and Lawton 1999)

From an ethical perspective, implementation issues focus both on the individual and the organization. In the first instance we might argue that by recruiting 'saints', unethical behaviour will simply not occur. More realistically we should attend to the organizational context. Thus, for example, the ICAC (1998) identifies a number of factors that inform an ethical culture:

- job satisfaction and commitment to the organization
- attitudes about the perceived values and behaviour of managers
- attitudes about the perceived values and behaviour of colleagues
- the perceived emphasis that the organization places on ethical behaviour
- trust and respect for supervisors, senior managers and colleagues
- risk factors of groupthink
- perceptions about the relationship between personal and organizational values.

There are few hard and concrete measures here, with a reliance on perceptions. The ICAC survey on ethical culture concluded that:

The ability to behave ethically in the workplace may be related more to aspects of the organization than to the attributes of the individual.

(ICAC 1998: 7)

and thus,

There is very little that managers can do to change an individual's personal moral beliefs. What managers can do is understand and change the factors specific to organizations which have been found to contribute to unethical decision-making in the workplace.

(ICAC 1998: 13)

If that is the case then we should concentrate on the organizational factors and eliminate risk and opportunity through building a concern with ethics into selection and promotion criteria; ethics training; codes of conduct; corruption prevention mechanisms; awareness training; ethical leadership; registers of interests, for example. Of course all of these may be abused where there is a climate which condones unethical behaviour. We examined ethical culture in Chapter 5 and an integrity approach in Chapter 7.

Another dimension to the implementation dynamics is that of unintended consequences and these may include:

- A sledgehammer to crack a nut – is it a question of overkill so that the creation of, say an all-singing and all-dancing anti-corruption agency might seem excessive to sort out a small number of petty frauds?
- Increased costs, finance and time such that the introduction of ethical regimes has to be borne often when public sector budgets are being cut.
- Increased bureaucratization in the form of the need to complete registers of interests or to develop appropriate procedures for dealing with complaints, etc.
- Organizational paralysis that inhibits innovation as well as an abdication of responsibility. It is possible for codes of conduct, for example, to be used as an excuse not to make a decision. Rather than using individual judgement there may be a tendency to consult the 'rule book' and as all incidences cannot be covered by a single rule then the rule book may proliferate.
- Tunnel vision, which focuses on that which is quantifiable.
- Because of the difficulties discussed above in defining performance there is a focus on a single measure such as a breach of a code of conduct. Not only that, but performance comes to be defined by what can be measured rather than by what ought to be measured.
- A 'tick box' mentality such that performance involves going through the motions, ensuring that minimum standards are met rather than evaluating whether it achieves anything. Thus we consider an organization to be ethical if it has a code of conduct and do not ask, 'But is it effective?'
- An overall reliance on statistics, league tables or other quantitative measures may mean that ethics becomes a game of manipulating statistics to ensure favourable reviews.
- Gaming by reporting on the successes and not the failures or by calling them something else. Gaming is similar to 'cream skimming' – don't report the problem areas, expel the problem kids, only treat 'healthy' patients to reduce waiting times in surgeries.

PERFORMANCE AND TRUST

Trust will be based on past performance, which informs expectations, and it is difficult to calculate the point at which people stop trusting others. Despite the introduction of ethical frameworks for local government and a general agreement upon principles of public life in the UK, a sceptical public remains to be convinced that elected politicians both at central and local levels can be trusted. Successive surveys carried out by opinion pollsters in the UK (see Table 8.3) show that doctors, teachers, the clergy and professors are the most trusted to tell the truth by the general public, while politicians generally rate just above tabloid journalists and estate agents at the bottom of the league table.

Different explanations are offered for the perceived decline in trust from a society point of view and these include post-modern explanations of changes in values to individualism, self-expression and self-fulfilment. Another explanation is the decline in social capital with the breakdown in communities. Interestingly, Van de Walle, Van Roosbroek and Bouckaert, after reviewing the large-scale

Table 8.3 *IPSOS MORI League Table*

Question: Would you tell me if you generally trust them to tell the truth or not?	% yes	% yes	% yes
Category	1993	2003	2011
Doctors	84	91	88
Teachers	84	87	81
Professors	70	74	74
Judges	68	72	72
Scientists	n/a	65	71
Clergymen/priests	80	71	68
The Police	63	64	63
Television news readers	72	66	62
Ordinary man/woman in the street	64	53	55
Civil servants	37	46	47
Pollsters	52	46	39
Trade union officials	32	33	34
Business leaders	32	28	29
Journalists	10	18	19
Government ministers	11	20	17
Politicians generally	14	18	14

Source IPSOS MORI/BMA (June 2011)

Base c. 1,000–2,000 British adults aged 15+

international data (World Values Survey)[1] argued that there is not a universal decline in trust in the public sector. Rather, we find fluctuations, not trends:

> Empirically, there is little evidence of an overall long-term decline in trust in government, although there are institutions that have suffered from a loss in trust.
>
> (Van de Walle *et al.* 2008: 61)

ETHICAL AUDIT

As Nutley (2000) argues, the faith placed in control by audit is associated with a declining trust in traditional forms of professional self-regulation. This is a theme first developed by Power (1997) who found audit valued as an article of faith, with routinized rituals of inspection:

> The audit society is not simply a distrusting society; rather, it reflects a tendency not to trust trust. This means a systemic tendency towards uncritical trust in the efficacy of audit processes, a trust which results in the absence of evaluation of the audit process itself.
>
> (Power 1997: 136–7)

Despite these problems associated with audit itself there is a growing interest in ethical audit. The modernization agenda for public services in the UK as defined in the Local Government Act (2000) included the development of an ethical framework as part of that agenda. Skelcher and Snape (2000) found that most local authorities concentrate on a narrow definition of an ethical framework which is about the creation of standards committees and adoption of the code of conduct. However, the extent to which such an approach might encourage ritualistic compliance where organizations go through the motions but behaviour does not change (Ashworth *et al.* 2002) is a moot point. A wider interpretation sees it as part of the overall approach to governance issues with an emphasis on prevention rather than cure or punishment. A small number of authorities are exploring the links between standards of conduct and audit. Individual local authorities are beginning to develop their own health checks for ethics, as we saw above with the London Borough Performance Indicators. Moreover, an ethical governance toolkit has been developed by the three agencies which exercised a major influence upon the ethical framework for local government (i.e. the Audit Commission, the Improvement and Development Agency (IDeA) and Standards for England). The three bodies combined to produce the toolkit, designed to be used in a number of stages, the initial stages being concerned with diagnosis, the responsibility of the Audit Commission, and the later stages with development, through the IDeA.

149

BOX 8.2   DISTRICT COUNCIL'S EXPERIENCE

District Council is an authority in the Midlands, which contains 19 town and parish councils. It has an active Monitoring Officer (Ethics Officer) who is a member of its senior management team and who regards ethical culture as crucially important to the authority's standing and performance. The Monitoring Officer initially decided to conduct an ethical audit and in order to facilitate the audit and to promote objectivity and good practice, District Council worked together with a neighbouring authority and with an external consultant. The audit was always regarded as a long-term project and was not intended to be a snapshot of the authority: 'we made it very clear that we were not doing this as a statistical exercise . . . it's not like auditing the council's books.' Furthermore there was commitment from all levels of management throughout the process.

The audit was conducted in three stages: an initial questionnaire looking at council documentation; a second diagnostic questionnaire; and follow-up training workshops. Despite the multi-method approach the audit was relatively straightforward and this was felt to be a key to its success: 'simplicity and clarity' are essential.

The audit was seen as a great success – so much so that the authority intends to conduct a version of it after every election. The audit did not uncover any specific problems within the authority but this was never its intention. The Monitoring Officer suggested that authority's experiencing any ethical problems should focus on them first and conduct an audit later. The process has not only raised awareness of ethical governance but has also had the concrete benefit of adding a new value – ethical governance – to the list of authorities' core values.

Commentary

The District Council's experience showed that despite the legitimizing nature of an external audit from an external body, there is no reason why a successful audit cannot be completed internally. The key value is commitment – especially if the process is going to be both long term and deeply rooted throughout the organization.

CONCLUSIONS

Measuring public service performance generally is difficult. External factors impact public service performance and these, by definition, are furthest from the control that can be exercised by the organization itself. Not only that, but those variables over which the organization can have some control, such as leadership, innovation, even strategy, do not demonstrate the same consistent pattern of improvement (Ashworth *et al.* 2002). Similarly with ethical performance, we do not have enough research evidence to argue that ethical leadership, or a code of conduct or training will have the greatest impact. We also do not know the impact of external regulation and inspection.

Yet, why a concern with ethics and why now? There are a number of different developments brought together under the ethics umbrella. One development is the perceived failure of traditional mechanisms of accountability such that there remain pockets of corrupt practices within the public services (e.g. expense scandals of UK MPs). Second, as part of the 'audit explosion' there is a political agenda that the mechanisms put in place to develop an ethical framework need to demonstrate their effectiveness. A third development is the growth in international concerns over widespread fraud and corruption.

Arguably, all the ethical audits in the world would not stop corrupt men and women from acting corruptly. Thus, is ethical audit another example of performance measurement gone mad? Or, should we recognize the failings of traditional accountability, believing that these failings are serious enough to warrant concern and that any attempt, no matter how inadequate, to improve ethical performance, is worth it? It is, perhaps, inevitable and understandable, that organizations will want to use an audit that compares them in a league table.

If the solution is ethical audit or review, as we prefer, then it needs to be recognized that a thin interpretation will not suffice. Review has to be not one task but several, e.g. technical, political, managerial and ethical, which is part of a wider ethical framework that includes awareness training, ethical guidelines and ethical decision-trees. Ethical audit has to reflect both individual performance and organizational setting and should consist of a number of different parts, including:

- prevention and anti-corruption measures
- values statements for the organization to aspire
- ethics awareness training
- personnel issues in terms of recruitment, promotion and appraisal
- leadership issues
- relationship issues in terms of, for example, trust
- public opinion.

151

The relationship between the individual, the organization and society is crucial. Is it possible to reconcile 'doing well' with 'doing good'? There has to be some agreement in values as a first step and there has to be recognition of the role of the public opinion, reflecting both isomorphism and democracy. The public ethos dimension needs to be reinvigorated as public services delivery increasingly relies on partnerships with a range of organizations including private sector ones.

Companies such as The Body Shop do demonstrate their social and public responsibility. The demands made on public service organizations should be greater, given that their reason for being is to serve the public interest, arrived at through democratic means and involving ethical considerations.

NOTE

1   http://www.worldvaluessurvey.org/

REFERENCES

Ashworth, R., Boyne, G.A. and Entwistle, T. (eds) (2010) *Public Service Improvement: Theories and Evidence*. Oxford: Oxford University Press.

Ashworth, R., Boyne, G.A. and Walker, R.M. (2002) 'Regulatory Problems in the Public Sector: Theories and Cases', *Policy and Politics* 30 (2): 195–211.

Barrett, S.M. (2004) 'Implementation Studies: Time For a Revival? Personal Reflections on 20 Years of Implementation Studies', *Public Administration* 82 (2): 249–62.

Bauman, Z. (1993) *Postmodern Ethics*. Oxford: Blackwell.

Behn, R. (2003) 'Why Measure Performance . . . ?' *Public Administration Review* 63 (5): 586–606.

Bekkers, V., Dijkstra, G., Edwards, A. and Fenger, M. (2007) *Governance and the Democratic Deficit: Assessing the Democratic Legitimacy of Governance Practices*. Aldershot: Ashgate Publishing.

Di Maggio, P.J. and Powell, W.W. (1991) (eds) *The New Institutionalism in Organizational Analysis*. Chicago, IL: University of Chicago Press.

Holloway, J. (1999) 'Managing Performance' in Rose, A. and Lawton, A. (eds) *Public Services Management*. London: Financial Times.

Hood, C., James, O., Jones, G., Scott, C. and Travers, T. (1998) 'Regulation Inside Government: Where New Public Management Meets the Audit Explosion', *Public Money & Management*, 18 (2): 61–8.

ICAC (1998) *Ethics: The Key to Good Management*. Sydney: ICAC.

IPOS MORI (2011) *IPOS MORI League Table*. British Medical Association.

Improvement and Development Agency (no date) 'Ethical Governance Audit'. London: IDeA.

Keohane, R.O. and Nye, J.S. (2001) *Power and Independence*. 3rd edition. New York: Longman.

Lawton, A. (1998) *Ethical Management for the Public Services*. Buckingham: Open University Press.

—— (2005) 'Public Service Ethics in a Changing World', *Futures* 37 (2–3): 231–43.

Maclagan, P. (1998) *Management and Morality: A Developmental Perspective*. London: Sage.

Noordegraaf, M. and Abma, T. (2003) 'Management by Measurement? Public Management Practices Amidst Ambiguity', *Public Administration* 81 (4): 853–71.

Nutley, S. (2000) 'Beyond Systems: HRM Audits in the Public Sector', *Human Resource Management Journal* 10 (2): 21–38.

OECD (2005) *Public Sector Integrity: A Framework for Assessment*. Paris: OECD.

—— (2009) *Towards a Sound Integrity Framework: Instruments, Processes, Structures and Conditions for Implementation*. Paris: OECD.

Power, M. (1997) *The Audit Society: Rituals of Verification*. Oxford: Oxford University Press.

Rose, A. and Lawton, A. (eds) (1999) *Public Services Management*. London: Financial Times Management.

Satava, D., Caldwell, C. and Richards, L. (2006) 'Ethics and the Auditing Culture: Rethinking the Foundation of Accounting and Auditing', *Journal of Business Ethics* 64 (3): 271–84.

Scharpf, F.W. (1999) *Governing in Europe: Effective and Democratic?* Oxford: Oxford University Press.

Schofield, J. (2004) 'A Model of Learned Implementation', *Public Administration* 82 (2): 283–308.

Skelcher, C. and Snape, S. (2000) *Political Executives and the New Ethical Framework*. DETR and IDeA.

Taylor, C. (1991) *The Ethics of Authenticity*. Cambridge, MA: Harvard University Press.

Thompson, D.F. (1980) 'Moral Responsibility of Public Officials: The Problem of Many Hands', *The American Political Science Review* 74 (4): 905–16.

Uhr, J. (1999) 'Institutions of Integrity: Balancing Values and Verification in Democratic Governance', *Public Integrity* 1 (1): 94–106.

Van de Walle, S., Van Roosbroek, S. and Bouckaert, G. (2008) 'Trust in the Public Sector: Is There Any Evidence for a Long-term Decline?', *International Review of Administrative Sciences* 74 (1): 47–64.

Chapter 9

Leadership
Does ethical leadership make a difference?

LEARNING OBJECTIVES

By the end of this chapter you should:

■ understand why and how public sector leaders are organizational key figures with regard to organizational ethics, i.e. ethical reasoning and (un)ethical behaviour of followers
■ understand the meaning and importance of ethical leadership
■ have examined some of the research evidence
■ have considered the effects of ethical leadership on organizational outcomes in contemporary contexts.

KEY POINTS IN THIS CHAPTER

■ Ethical leadership is a multi-dimensional concept – distinct from other leadership styles consisting of the components 'the moral person', 'the moral manager' and a 'positive leader–follower relationship'.
■ Several theories – cognitive moral development theory, social learning theory, reinforcement theory and social exchange theory – explain the role that leaders have in organizations with regard to ethics and integrity.
■ For building a reputation as an ethical leader, both the moral person and the moral manager need to be equally strong. Public sector leaders often underestimate the latter, and thereby risk being perceived as ethically neutral leaders.

- Ethical leadership contributes to an ethical climate and many other positive organizational outcomes, and although it seems a good overall leadership strategy, it is not a panacea.
- Ethical leadership can be considered as a variform universal concept; while the basic components of ethical leadership – moral person, moral manager, positive leader–follower relationship – may be rather consistent across different types of organizations, the way these components are interpreted and enacted may differ, as may the relative weight that people give to the respective components. Ethical leadership in practice might depend on the organizational, cultural or societal context.
- Ethical leadership is not exclusively reserved for managers; hence, it might be found at all levels within an organization.

KEY TERMS

Ethical leadership – 'the demonstration of normatively appropriate conduct through personal actions and interpersonal relationships, and promotion of such conduct among followers through two-way communication, reinforcement, and decision-making processes' (Brown, Treviño and Harrison 2005: 120).

INTRODUCTION

Managers are people who do things right and leaders are people who do the right thing.

Bennis and Nanus (1985: 21)

In several chapters of this book we referred to the role of leadership and managers, for instance in cultivating public service motivation (Chapter 4) or fostering an ethical climate (Chapter 5). Much has been said and written about leadership (on the internet you will be bombarded with millions of hits if you search the keyword *leadership*!), and there are almost as many ways to define leadership as there are persons who have attempted to define it (Bass 1990). In this chapter we will investigate the role of leadership for organizational ethics. To conceptualize leadership in terms of the styles and behaviours that seem important for this topic, we will concentrate on *ethical* leadership and mainly leave other leadership and management insights aside.

A key aim of this chapter is to gain a greater understanding of ethical leadership and the role it potentially plays in fostering an ethical climate in public sector organizations. In doing this we have considered some of the growing research around the subject and gained insight into the extent to which it is a universal concept. This chapter considers what ethical leadership is, and why and how ethical leaders are important in safeguarding ethics and integrity in organizations. In particular, it discusses the relationship between ethical leadership and ethical reasoning and ethical behaviour of followers.

WHY AND HOW ARE LEADERS IMPORTANT FOR ORGANIZATIONAL ETHICS?

Several theories explain why and how leaders are important to the ethical reasoning and ethical behaviour of their employees ('followers'). In terms of why, Kohlberg's (1976) cognitive moral development theory, discussed in Chapter 2, suggests that leaders, especially immediate supervisors, can be a key source of moral guidance for employees who look outside themselves to rules, laws and authority figures.

In contrast, social learning theory, reinforcement theory and social exchange theory focus more on how leaders can influence their followers' integrity. The social learning theory as developed by Bandura (1977) points out that leaders can transmit values, attitudes and behaviours by way of modelling and identification processes, thereby leading by example and serving as role models for their employees (e.g. Ford and Richardson 1994; Lewis 1991). To put it simply: employees are likely to imitate their supervisors and will learn what to do, as well as what not to do, by observing their leaders' behaviour. Somewhat differently, reinforcement theory suggests that individual behaviour is a result of its prospective consequences; for instance leaders can steer employees' behaviour through specific rewards and punishments (Treviño 1986). Moreover, by doing so, employees themselves become role models for other employees whose behaviour leaders either reward or punish.

Social exchange theory, on the other hand, argues that followers' ethical behaviour is influenced by the quality of the interpersonal treatment that employees receive from leaders; the better the treatment, the more employees feel themselves obliged to reciprocate positive behaviours (Treviño and Brown 2005). In the next section these underlying theories become clear in the conceptualization of the ethical leader.

THE CONCEPT OF ETHICAL LEADERSHIP

To investigate the meanings of ethical leadership, Ciulla (2004) proposes that the ethics of leadership be examined along five interlinked dimensions: (1) the ethics of a leader as a person; (2) the ethics of the leader/follower relationship; (3) the ethics of the process of leadership; (4) the ethics of what a leader does or does not do; and (5) the ethics of leadership in the larger context of the community. See Exercise 9.1.

EXERCISE 9.1 CONCEPTUALIZING ETHICAL LEADERS

Think of a supervisor (or manager/leader) of a public service organization that you either work(ed) for or have experienced.

How important would you say he or she is for you and your co-workers in terms of moral guidance? What does (s)he teach you about organizational ethics and which moral values, norms and rules do you follow? And how does (s)he make that happen (through role-modelling, specific rewards and punishments, the quality of the interpersonal treatment)?

One way of defining ethical leadership, which relates to all these dimensions, is found in the work of Brown *et al.* (2005: 120):

> [Ethical leadership is] the demonstration of normatively appropriate conduct through personal actions and interpersonal relationships, and promotion of such conduct among followers through two-way communication, reinforcement, and decision-making processes.

The first part of this definition suggests that ethical leaders are perceived by their followers as credible role models for how to behave, and points out the importance of maintaining high-quality relationships. Nonetheless, 'normative appropriate conduct' might in reality be context-dependent. In fact, as we discussed earlier in this book, values and norms differ between public and private sector organizations or between cultures and countries.

The second part implies that ethical leaders not only talk frequently about ethics and promote ethical behaviour, but also provide their followers with a voice. Finally, the term 'reinforcement' implies that ethical leaders set ethical standards, reward ethical conduct, and discipline unethical conduct; while the phrase 'decision-making processes' suggests that ethical leaders consider the ethical consequences of their decisions and make principled and fair choices that are visible for others (cf. Brown *et al.* 2005). As this definition implies, the primary objective of ethical leadership is to cultivate ethical reasoning and behaviour among followers and it is this explicit focus on promoting and managing ethics that distinguishes ethical leadership from other leadership styles such as transformational (see, for example, Bass and Steidlmeier 1999) or authentic leadership (see, for example, Avolio and Gardner 2005). In addition, other scholars that describe ethical leadership also stress the morality of the leader's character, vision and the morality of leadership–follower processes, but fail to explicitly shed light on the active role and ethical obligations of leaders. This is illustrated by the following definition:

157

The ethics of leadership rests upon three pillars: (1) the moral character of the leader; (2) the ethical legitimacy of the values embedded in the leader's vision, articulation, and program which followers either embrace or reject; and (3) the morality of the processes of social ethical choice and action that leaders and followers engage in and collectively pursue.

(Bass and Steidlmeier 1999: 182)

More specifically, ethical leadership may be conceived as consisting of three fundamental components, as illustrated in Figure 9.1. The first concerns the personal integrity and moral character of the leader, also termed the 'moral person'

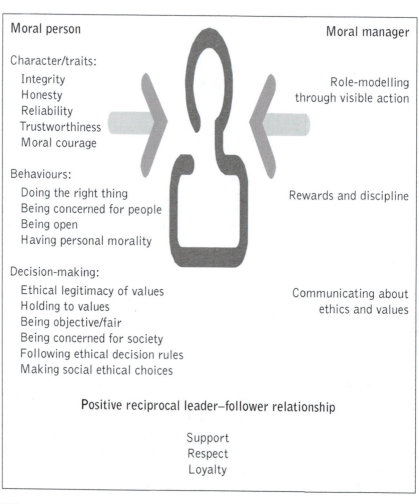

Figure 9.1 *The pillars of ethical leadership*

Source: based on Treviño, Hartman and Brown (2000: 131)

component of ethical leadership. The second emphasizes the extent to which a leader is able to cultivate integrity among his or her followers; that is, the 'moral manager' component (Treviño, Hartman and Brown 2000). The third component concerns the quality of the leader–follower relationship, which bridges the moral person and the moral manager components and which reflects their effects on followers (cf. Heres and Lasthuizen, forthcoming a).

THE MORAL PERSON

When thinking of an ethical leader, you probably think of a person with high morals, like Mahatma Ghandi or Martin Luther King Jr., and indeed most theoretical and empirical studies stress that ethical leadership is first and foremost grounded in the leaders' personal moral values and their moral courage to uphold these values and principles, even in the face of significant external pressures, adversity or risks. Similarly, ethical leadership is associated with personal traits such as integrity, honesty, reliability and trustworthiness (or other 'moral' qualities you can think of, which we do not mention here to avoid an endless list). In the leaders' behaviour such traits should become especially visible in a heightened awareness of others: ethical leaders are open, people-oriented, caring and have a genuine interest in others' well-being (Brown and Treviño 2006). This concern for others also expresses itself in a heightened awareness of the context in which one operates (Avolio and Gardner 2005). Ethical leaders act in accordance with the broader common good (Michie and Gooty 2005; Resick et al. 2006; Treviño, Brown and Hartman 2003; Van Wart 2005), and although they lead others, a point we discuss in the next section, they themselves need not be exceptionally charismatic or visionary people (Treviño et al. 2003). The 'moral person' component of ethical leadership is also inherently embedded in the leader's decision-making. In fact, some of the earliest empirical research on ethical leadership, concern studies on leaders' (or managers') ethical decision-making and behaviour (e.g. Fritzsche and Becker 1984). Ethical leaders are able to recognize the moral elements of the decision and oversee the moral consequences of their decisions, the end goals they set and the means used to achieve them (Turner et al. 2002; Wittmer 1992). Subsequently, ethical leaders must be 'capable of judging ambiguous ethical issues, viewing them from multiple perspectives, and aligning decisions with their own moral values' (Brown and Treviño 2006: 599). Ethical leaders need to be ethically competent (cf. Menzel 2009), meaning that ethical leaders are able to make balanced ethical decisions, incorporating such steps as we described in Chapter 7 in the ethical decision-making model (see Figure 7.1.)

Finally, ethical leaders must make efforts to remain consistent in their decision-making and behaviour (Kaptein 2003; Van Wart 2005): they need to 'walk the talk and talk the walk' (Brown and Treviño 2006; Davis and Rothstein 2006; Palanski and Yammarino 2009). The moral person component can be thought of as the ethical part of the term 'ethical leadership'. However, simply being an ethical person does not necessarily tell employees what they should do. The second moral manager component does, and hence mirrors the leader in 'ethical leadership' (cf. Heres and Lasthuizen, forthcoming a).

THE MORAL MANAGER

As pictured in Figure 9.1, the 'moral manager' component of ethical leadership is composed of three key elements: leaders' role-modelling through visible action, rewards and discipline, and communication about ethics and values (Brown, Treviño and Harrison 2005). Of these, leader role-modelling is shown to be the most critical factor in shaping the ethical reasoning and ethical behaviour of employees (Lasthuizen 2008; Menzel 2007; Neubert et al. 2009; Treviño et al. 1999). For leaders, therefore, it is important to think about how to set the ethical tone in an organization and make their ethical role-modelling sufficiently visible and salient to their employees. Especially role-modelling ethical behaviour is essential for effective reinforcement and communication on ethics, as it conveys the underlying principles that leaders themselves adhere to and thereby directly attests to the credibility of the leader. If leaders lack such credibility, their words simply lose power (Simons 1999); and without visible ethical role-modelling, leaders might be perceived as ethically neutral (Treviño et al. 2003). In other words, to develop a reputation for ethical leadership, a leader must be strong on both the moral person and the moral manager dimension. In Figure 9.2 this idea

strong MORAL MANAGER weak	Hypocritical leader	Ethical leader
	Unethical leader	Ethically neutral leader
	weak MORAL PERSON strong	

Figure 9.2 *Executive reputation and ethical leadership*

Source: based on Treviño et al. (2000: 137)

is visualized in four types of leaders: hypocritical leaders, unethical leaders, ethically neutral leaders and ethical leaders.

On the other hand, ethical leaders should be careful not to send out negative or conflicting signals: just as a good example may encourage employees to join in, they might also copy a bad example, even if this was not intentionally done (Jurkiewicz and Thompson 1999; Den Hartog and De Hoogh 2009; Kaptein 2003). Unethical leadership harms the organization more than passive leadership (Lasthuizen 2008). It is therefore essential to reflect on how to be an ethical role model and be aware of how decisions and behaviours are perceived and might be interpreted by followers: '[People] are generally not aware of our intent. They see the actions and make inferences based upon them' (Treviño *et al.* 2000: 134).

A second element of the 'moral manager' is holding people accountable for their conduct and reinforcing ethical standards through reward and discipline. This is important because employees are more likely to do what is rewarded and avoid doing what is punished (Kaptein and Wempe 2002; Ball, Trevino and Sims 1994; Treviño 1992). If unethical behaviour, intentionally or not is left unpunished, facilitated, or even rewarded it might be perceived as acceptable behaviour and continue in the future. As a Dutch Chief Commissioner of the Police said: 'Everything you just walk by, you implicitly approve.'

Likewise, compliance-based programmes (see Chapters 6 and 7) and too much emphasis on formal sanctions and rewards might lead to employees who do not think autonomously, merely doing what is asked of them. As a result, this may actually lower their level of moral reasoning and provide them with a justification for not considering the broader implications their actions and those of the organization may have for various stakeholders (Baucus and Beck-Dudley 2005; Paine 1994; Roberts 2009). Rewards such as recognition, trust and respect, increased discretion and autonomy, status and power, will also encourage employees to behave ethically and refrain from unethical behaviour (Grojean *et al.* 2004; Treviño 1992). Even more, if rewards and discipline are made readily visible and explained to others in the organization, the learning experience of reinforcement lies not just with the person(s) being rewarded or punished, but also occurs vicariously and anticipatory among those that observe the reinforcement actions of the leader (cf. Lasthuizen 2008).

The third key aspect of the 'moral manager' component of ethical leadership concerns communication about ethics and values. Ethical leaders speak about what is right and what is wrong, what is permitted and what is forbidden (Brown 2007). It seems self-evident that communication about the true meaning of integrity in the organization is essential. Openness to talk about and discuss integrity stimulates employees to comply and helps to instil values that promote a commitment to ethical conduct. Such communication entails highlighting the ethical dimension of decisions, tasks and situations, clarifying norms and role expectations, and

161

providing guidance on the appropriate course of action (Cooper 2006; De Hoogh and Den Hartog 2008; Van den Akker *et al.* 2009). Additionally, ethical leaders communicate their ethics message by making their own decision-making processes transparent (see the decision-making model in Figure 7.1). This includes being open about alternatives and the principles and justifications that underlie the final decision made (Grundstein-Amado 1999; Piccolo *et al.* 2010; Weaver, Treviño and Agle 2005). Of course, communication about ethics and values is not just sending a one-directional message; it entails a two-way interaction between leaders and followers. Leaders are therefore encouraged to be open, approachable and willing to listen to their followers and to provide them with feedback regarding their ethical conduct (Huberts, Kaptein and Lasthuizen 2007). They need to create an environment in which followers feel comfortable and safe to talk to their leader and co-workers about ethics, to discuss the ethical dilemmas they are confronted with and ask for advice, to be honest about the mistakes they have made, and willing to report problems and deliver bad news to the leader (Brown *et al.* 2005). By doing so, employees start to think independently and creatively, to critically question their own and the organization's assumptions, and to examine their modes of thinking. As we have discussed in Chapter 7, this is in line with an integrity-based approach, which is assumed to be more effective because it is rooted in self-governance. Leaders can help to encourage such a type of ethical climate by being open and honest about their own ethical dilemmas and decision-making because they show that it is acceptable and even encouraged to bring ethical issues to the fore (Heres and Lasthuizen, forthcoming b).

THE RELATIONSHIP BETWEEN LEADER AND FOLLOWER

In the most fundamental sense, leadership can simply be described as some type of relation between leader and follower. As McCall (2002: 133) notes:

> 'leader' is an achievement term that denotes some degree of success in eliciting collective behaviour from others in pursuit of a goal to be achieved and 'leading' is taken to require some level of buy-in by followers to the leader's goals and methods, strategies and tactics.

Therefore, the last component of ethical leadership that is important to discuss, concerns the relationship between the leader and his or her employees. This relationship can be considered as the basis of the ethical leadership framework (see Figure 9.1). The way ethical leaders treat their followers is the basis for making things actually happen. It is not merely a matter of the leader's personal integrity, but in fact partly accounts for leaders' ability to arouse ethical decision-making and behaviour amongst followers. Especially by drawing on social exchange theory and the norm of reciprocity (Gouldner 1960), it has been shown that when leaders treat their employees fairly and when they are supportive of and loyal to their subordinates, they are more likely to be reciprocated with the desired ethical behaviour and less likely to be confronted with unethical behaviour of their followers (Den Hartog and De Hoogh 2009; Mayer *et al.* 2009; Neubert *et al.* 2009; Resick *et al.* 2006). Furthermore, a fair and just interpersonal treatment of employees fosters the feeling of attachment to leaders, thereby elevating their moral authority status and enhancing the motivation of followers to emulate their behaviour (Detert *et al.* 2007; Neubert *et al.* 2009). Or to put it more simply: treating others the way you want to be treated yourself makes it easier to become an ethical leader, to be a credible role model, and to foster an ethical climate.

WHAT ABOUT UNETHICAL LEADERSHIP?

So far we have paid attention to what is needed for being an ethical leader, but what makes a leader an unethical leader? Scoring low on the ethical leadership components and characteristics described above does not necessarily mean that a leader is unethical; it might be the case that such a leader is not visibly an ethical leader (see Figure 9.2). Thus, if ethical leadership is embodied by leaders that display ethical conduct and promote the ethics and integrity of followers, then conversely, unethical leadership can be thought of as referring to leaders that display unethical conduct and discourage employee ethics and integrity (Craig and Gustafson 1998). For example, Van Wart (2006: 39) suggests that the most common symptom of unethical leadership styles is that leaders 'use their positions for their personal benefit or for a special group at the expense of others'. Obviously it is often much easier to think of leaders who fail the ethics test, and this seems to hold especially for political leaders. An example is Silvio Berlusconi, former prime minister of Italy who was accused of many unethical and illegal practices such as corruption and bribery; conflicts of interest; links to the mafia; abuse of media for political gain as well as sex scandals. However, he managed to stay in office until November 2011 when he was ultimately forced to step down. A positive example of ethical leadership is the current president of Liberia, Ellen Johnson Sirleaf, who was awarded the Nobel Peace Prize in 2011. *Newsweek* and *Time* listed her as one of the ten best (female) leaders in the world, while *The Economist* described her as arguably the best president the country has ever had.

To evaluate ethical leadership of leaders in public sector organizations at all levels, whether it may be an immediate supervisor, middle manager or CEO, go to Exercise 9.2 and consider Table 9.1, which provides a questionnaire to tap ethical and unethical leadership.

EXERCISE 9.2   ETHICAL LEADERSHIP

Think of a supervisor (or manager/leader) of a public service organization that you either work(ed) for or have experienced.

Look at the questionnaire (Table 9.1) and answer by ticking off one of the options, 'disagree', 'neutral' or 'agree'.

How often did you tick 'agree' for the ethical leadership items and how often did you tick 'disagree' for the unethical leadership items? What room is left for improvement of the ethical leadership within your organization?

Commentary

In answering these questions and reflecting on the overall outcome, you may like to think about some of the following points. In this chapter we illustrate the ethical leader and discuss the corresponding key components. The items above give you concrete questions to recognize behaviours of ethical leadership or unethical leadership in organizational practice. However, as demonstrated in Figure 9.2, managers themselves, whether in the public sector, hybrid or private sector organizations, are often insufficiently aware of the notion that they need to build a reputation of an ethical leader. In order to be perceived as an ethical leader, the 'moral manager' dimension should be as strongly developed as the one of the 'moral person', which is often overlooked. Finally, one must know that in order to create a strong ethical environment, most of the items described above do not only apply to managers, but to employees as well. You might want to fill out the questionnaire for your co-workers and last, but not least, for yourself.

THE EFFECTS OF ETHICAL LEADERSHIP ON ORGANIZATIONAL OUTCOMES

So far we have discussed the meaning of ethical leadership. In this section we describe the importance of ethical leadership. Empirical research shows that ethical leadership can have numerous positive outcomes. At the very least, organizational ethical leadership limits counterproductive behaviour of employees and fosters an ethical climate (Avey, Palanski and Walumbwa 2010; De Hoogh and Den Hartog 2008; Lasthuizen 2008; Mayer et al. 2009). Results from previous research indicates that followers of ethical leaders have a higher capacity of ethical reasoning (Lasthuizen 2008), have less intentions to commit unethical acts (Chou et al. 2010) and, accordingly, display less behaviour that violates ethical norms and values (Treviño et al. 2003).

Table 9.1 *Questionnaire for ethical leadership*

	Disagree	Neutral	Agree
Ethical leadership			
My supervisor sets a good example in terms of ethical behaviour			
My supervisor meets his/her obligations			
My supervisor does what s/he says			
My supervisor clarifies which values and norms should be lived up to			
My supervisor communicates the importance of ethics and integrity well			
My supervisor makes sure that his/her actions are always ethical			
My supervisor would never authorize unethical or illegal conduct to meet organizational goals			
My supervisor takes reports of undesirable employee conduct seriously			
My supervisor is accessible to me to discuss moral dilemmas in the task performance			
My supervisor will appreciate it that, if I have to do something that conflicts with my conscience, I discuss this with him/her			
My supervisor is alert to potentially undesirable behaviour within my work unit			
My supervisor will appreciate it that, if a colleague acts unethically, I discuss this with him/her			
My supervisor will call me or a colleague to account if s/he observes us behaving unethically			
My supervisor sanctions someone who consciously behaves unethically			
Unethical leadership			
My supervisor does not behave in a manner consistent with the values s/he expresses			
My supervisor manipulates subordinates			
My supervisor holds me responsible for things that are not my fault			
My supervisor acts without considering my feelings			

Lasthuizen's study (2008) indicates that ethical role-modelling of public sector leaders is especially effective in minimizing integrity violations that relate to interpersonal relationships within the organization, including bullying, sexual harassment, or gossiping about colleagues. But when it comes to integrity violations that concern organizational resources (e.g. misuse of working hours for private purposes, falsely calling in sick or carelessness in the use of organizational resources), it is essential that a leader is strict and reinforces behaviour through rewards and punishments. And, finally, clarifying ethical values and norms and being open to discuss ethical dilemmas seem most effective in reducing favouritism within the organization and discrimination of the public outside the organization (see Huberts *et al.* 2007).

It is important here to notice that the effect that ethical leadership has on (un)ethical behaviour goes above and beyond the effect of other, more general leadership styles without a specific focus on ethics (Brown *et al.* 2005; Lasthuizen 2008). Additionally, ethical leadership appears to be beneficial beyond ethics as well as it equally has positive effects on other than ethical organizational outcomes as well. Consider Box 9.1 in which we give an overview of empirical findings (Heres and Lasthuizen, forthcoming a).

The reason for such positive outcomes of ethical leadership may lie in findings that indicate that employees are more satisfied with leaders that they see as ethical leaders, but perhaps even more notably, they also consider ethical leaders to be more effective (Brown *et al.* 2005; see also Parry and Proctor-Thomson 2002). In

BOX 9.1 ORGANIZATIONAL OUTCOMES OF ETHICAL LEADERSHIP

- Less unethical behaviour of employees
- Employees have a higher level of ethical reasoning
- Fosters an ethical organizational climate (see Chapter 5)
- Makes employees feel that their work is more meaningful
- Makes employees feel like they have more control over their job
- Employees take more initiative and put in extra effort
- Employees are more altruistic and show more willingness to help others with work-related problems
- Stimulates Organizational Citizenship Behaviour (OCB; see Chapter 4)
- Employees have more dedication to work and a better work attitude
- Employees exhibit more self-efficacy and are less uncertain
- Employees have a more optimistic view of the future
- Cultivates trust in and lessens interpersonal conflicts between co-workers
- More identification with and commitment to the organization

sum, ethical leadership improves the overall performance of followers and therefore seems to be a good overall leadership strategy (Khuntia and Suar 2004; Walumbwa *et al.* 2011).

Importantly, although ethical leadership has been found to be positively related to organizational ethics, it should be noted that the influence between ethical leadership and ethical behaviour primarily works indirectly and is not a merely one-to-one effect. Ethical leadership contributes to employee behaviour through the ethical organizational culture and by influencing employee ethical reasoning, and therefore ethical leadership is neither an instant solution nor a panacea to all problems and troubles (cf. Lasthuizen 2008). Ethical leadership is probably best seen as a crucial layer between organizational ethical values and norms, which are embedded in ethics policies and programmes, on the one hand, and an ethical climate and employee ethical reasoning and behaviour on the other hand.

ETHICAL LEADERSHIP IN DIFFERENT CONTEXTS

Before concluding this chapter we pay some attention to recent research that suggests that ethical leadership is a variform universal concept. To date, research on ethical leadership has been rather inattentive to the nature of the organizational context within which ethical leadership is exerted, implicitly assuming that a 'one size fits all' solution is adequate for organizations operating in different environments, societies or cultures. Also the way in which ethical leadership is measured in empirical studies, for instance, with standardized surveys and item batteries, is little sensitive to its contingencies (e.g. the ten-item EL scale of Brown *et al.* 2005). An important theory in this respect is the implicit leadership theory of which the starting point is that 'leadership is in the eye of the beholder'. Everyone has implicit ideas or beliefs about what a leader looks like, what characteristics he or she has and how he or she behaves. Thus, an ethical leader is someone who matches such an implicit set of beliefs. People in the same group, whether this is an organization, a culture or a society at large, will share more similar notions and beliefs than outsiders. Additionally, beliefs about different kinds of leaders within groups may well exist. Nonetheless, the question of which environments differ for the belief set of a leader has not been extensively researched to date. Whether there is one best way to be an ethical leader or whether this is in fact context-dependent, remains largely unknown. To test the assumption of implicit leadership theories, see Exercise 9.3.

There are a few studies that claim that the scope of ethical leadership should be expanded to be able to take into account the contextual differences that may occur in the conceptions and manifestations of ethical leadership. Studies on implicit leadership theories, like the Global Leadership and Organizational Behaviour Effectiveness study (GLOBE) (see Den Hartog *et al.* 1999, Resick *et al.* 2006), have shown consistently that notions on what leadership in general and ethical

EXERCISE 9.3   EXPECTATIONS OF LEADERS

Think of one political leader, one public sector leader, one business leader and one leader in sports.

■ What do you expect from the ethical leadership of these various leaders? (See Figure 9.1.)

■ Should they all behave the same or do your expectations in how they will behave differ?

■ Is it, for example, more permissible for a political leader to be unethical in the political arena?

■ What type of leader do you expect to be the best moral manager?

■ And, does that matter for all types of leaders in terms of being a hypocritical, unethical, ethically neutral or ethical leader?

■ Do you think that the ethical leadership beliefs and expectations of public sector employees in India are the same as those of employees in Belgium or in Australia?

leadership in particular entails are culture-dependent and influence the extent to which particular leadership characteristics and behaviours are effective in influencing follower behaviour. Van den Akker *et al.* (2009) showed in a survey among employees of a multinational enterprise that for an ethical leader to be effective, he or she has to fulfil their employees' expectations regarding how they believe that ethical leadership should be fulfilled in their work environment. In a similar vein, both the studies of Lasthuizen (2008) and De Hoogh and Den Hartog (2008) indicate that the various aspects and components of ethical leadership differ in their respective effects on follower behaviours. Recent findings in an exploratory study among public, hybrid and private sector leaders (Heres and Lasthuizen, forthcoming b) indicate that existing conceptions of ethical leadership as a universally applicable, mono-dimensional construct may not be adequate: subtle differences were found in leaders' views on ethical leadership depending on the type of sector. For instance, private sector leaders placed more emphasis on honesty, while public and hybrid sector leaders emphasized that ethical leadership requires an outward, societal focus, which is in line with the very nature of the organizational tasks and mission, and to the public service motivation of their employees (see Chapter 4). Moreover, in public and hybrid sector organizations, ethical leadership should frequently address ethics-related issues and leaders should explicitly communicate in terms like 'ethics' and 'integrity', whereas in private sector organizations, leaders often wanted to avoid these terms and preferred to use more implicit communication strategies. In addition, a gender effect was found. Female leaders seemed to emphasize empathy and care in ethical leadership more than male leaders. It seems then that ethical leadership is perhaps best understood as a variform universal phenomenon: the general principles and components of ethical leadership (moral person, moral manager, positive leader–follower relationship) are universally stable, yet the precise meaning and enactment of those principles and components vary across contexts (Heres and Lasthuizen, forthcoming b; cf. Bass 1997). You could imagine this in various profiles of ethical leaders – that each is somewhat different in their precise outlook and dealings with ethical issues in their daily practice.

CONCLUSIONS

To summarize, this chapter has discussed why leaders are organizational key figures with regard to organizational ethics and how they can provide moral guidance to their followers. We have defined ethical leadership and identified the three essential components: moral person, moral manager and a positive leader–follower relationship that together constitute ethical leadership in organizations. Furthermore, we gave two examples of (un)ethical leadership in politics to illustrate the importance of building a reputation as an ethical leader and a way of measuring ethical leadership in organizations. We have presented a range of positive outcomes resulting from deploying ethical leadership, in public sector organizations and beyond, although we stressed that the importance of ethical leadership alone should not be exaggerated. You have been encouraged to think about ethical leadership as a variform universal phenomenon, although to date only few comparative studies have been conducted to verify the idea that ethical leadership might indeed be partly context-dependent.

In the meantime, we propose that managers, individuals and organizations have a role to play in cultivating ethics and integrity by means of ethical leadership. This includes your own role as well: you might want to take the lead, place ethics at the forefront of your attentions and start by setting a good example to others in your environment.

REFERENCES

Avey, J.B., Palanski, M.E. and Walumbwa, F.O. (2010) 'When Leadership Goes Unnoticed: The Moderating Role of Follower Self-esteem on the Relationship Between Ethical Leadership and Follower Behavior', *Journal of Business Ethics* 98 (4): 573–82.

Avolio, B.J. and Gardner, W.L. (2005) 'Authentic Leadership Development: Getting to the Root of Positive Forms of Leadership', *The Leadership Quarterly* 16 (3): 315–38.

Ball, G.A., Trevino, L.K. and Sims, H.P. (1994) 'Just and Unjust Punishment: Influences on Subordinate Performance and Citizenship', *Academy of Management Journal* 37 (2): 299–322.

Bandura, A. (1977) *Social Learning Theory*. New York: General Learning Press.

Bass, B.M. (1990) *Bass and Stogdill's Handbook of Leadership: Theory, Research and Managerial Applications*. 3rd edition. New York: Free Press.

—— (1997) 'Does the Transactional-Transformational Leadership Paradigm Transcend Organisational and National Boundaries?' *American Psychologist* 52 (2): 130–9.

Bass, B.M. and Steidlmeier, P. (1999) 'Ethics, Character, and Authentic Trans-formational Leadership Behavior', *The Leadership Quarterly* 10 (2): 181–217.

Baucus, M.S. and Beck-Dudley, C.L. (2005) 'Designing Ethical Organizations: Avoiding the Long-term Negative Effects of Rewards and Punishments', *Journal of Business Ethics* 56 (4): 355–70.

Bennis, W. and Nanus, B. (1985) *Leaders: The Strategies for Taking Charge*. New York: Harper & Row.

Brown, M.E. (2007) 'Misconceptions of Ethical Leadership: How to Avoid Potential Pitfalls', *Organizational Dynamics* 36 (2): 140–55.

Brown, M.E. and Treviño, L.K. (2006) 'Ethical Leadership: A Review and Future Directions', *The Leadership Quarterly* 17 (6): 595–616.

Brown, M.E., Treviño, L.K. and Harrison, D.A. (2005) 'Ethical Leadership: A Social Learning Perspective for Construct Development and Testing', *Organizational Behavior and Human Decision Processes* 97 (2): 117–34.

Chou, L.-F., Tseng, C.-J., Yeh, H.-C.D. and Chiang, Y.-M. (2010) 'Perceived Environmental Uncertainty, Sales Performance and Unethical Intention: Leader-ship Matters?' Paper presented at *Academy of Management Meeting*, Montréal, Canada, August 6–10, 2010.

Ciulla, J.B. (2004) 'The Relationship of Ethics to Effectiveness in Leadership' in Sternberg, R.J., Antonakis, J. and Cianciolo, A.T. (eds) *The Nature of Leadership*. Thousand Oaks, CA, London and New Delhi: Sage Publications, pp. 302–27.

Cooper, T.L. (2006) *The Responsible Administrator: An Approach to Ethics for the Administrative Role*. 5th edition. San Francisco, CA: Jossey-Bass.

Craig, S.B. and Gustafson, S.B. (1998) 'Perceived Leader Integrity Scale: An Instrument for Assessing Employee Perceptions of Leader Integrity', *The Leadership Quarterly* 9 (2): 127–45.

Davis, A.L. and Rothstein H.R. (2006) 'The Effects of the Perceived Behavioral Integrity of Managers on Employee Attitudes: A Meta-analysis', *Journal of Business Ethics* 67 (4): 407–19.

De Hoogh, A.H.B. and Den Hartog, D.N. (2008) 'Ethical and Despotic Leadership, Relationships with Leader's Social Responsibility, Top Management Team Effectiveness and Subordinates' Optimism: A Multi-method Study', *The Leadership Quarterly* 19 (3): 297–311.

Den Hartog, D.N. and De Hoogh, A.H.B. (2009) 'Empowering Behaviour and Leader Fairness and Integrity: Studying Perceptions of Ethical Leader Behaviour from a

Levels-of-analysis Perspective', *European Journal of Work and Organizational Psychology* 18 (2): 199–230.

Den Hartog, D.N., House, R.J., Hanges, P.J. and Ruiz-Quintanilla, S.A. (1999) 'Culture Specific and Cross-culturally Generalizable Implicit Leadership Theories: Are Attributes of Charismatic/Transformational Leadership Universally Endorsed?' *The Leadership Quarterly* 10 (2): 219–56.

Detert, J.R., Treviño, L.K., Burris, E.R. and Andiappan, M. (2007) 'Managerial Modes of Influence and Counterproductivity in Organizations: A Longitudinal Business-unit-level Investigation', *Journal of Applied Psychology* 92 (4): 993–1005.

Ford, R.C. and Richardson, W.D. (1994) 'Ethical Decision-making: A Review of the Empirical Literature', *Journal of Business Ethics* 13 (3): 205–21.

Fritzsche, D.J. and Becker, H. (1984) 'Linking Management Behavior to Ethical Philosophy: An Empirical Investigation', *Academy of Management Journal* 27 (1): 166–75.

Gouldner, A.W. (1960) 'The Norm of Reciprocity', *American Sociological Review* 25 (2): 161–78.

Grojean, M., Resick, C., Dickson, M. and Smith, D. (2004). 'Leaders, Values, and Organizational Climate: Examining Leadership Strategies for Establishing an Organizational Climate Regarding Ethics', *Journal of Business Ethics* 55 (3): 223–41.

Grundstein-Amado, R. (1999) 'Bilateral Transformational Leadership – An Approach for Fostering Ethical Conduct in Public Service Organizations', *Administration & Society* 31 (2): 247–60.

Heres, L. and Lasthuizen, K. (forthcoming a) 'From Ethical Competence to Ethical Leadership' in Menzel, D.C. and Cooper, T.L. (eds) *Achieving Ethical Competence for Public Service Leadership.* New York: M.E. Sharpe, pp. 77–100.

Heres, L. and Lasthuizen, K. (forthcoming b) 'What's the Difference? Ethical Leadership in Public, Hybrid, and Private Sector Organisations'. Special issue of the *Journal of Change Management.*

Huberts, L.W.J.C., Kaptein, M. and Lasthuizen, K. (2007) 'A Study of the Impact of Three Leadership Styles on Integrity Violations Committed by Police Officers', *Policing: An International Journal of Police Strategies & Management* 30 (4): 587–607.

Jurkiewicz, C.L. and Thompson, C.R. (1999) 'An Empirical Inquiry into the Ethical Standards of Health Care Administrators', *Public Integrity* 1 (1): 41–53.

Kaptein, M. (2003) 'The Diamond of Managerial Integrity', *European Management Review* 21 (1): 99–108.

Kaptein, M. and Wempe, J. (2002) *The Balanced Company: A Theory of Corporate Integrity.* Oxford: Oxford University Press.

Khuntia, R. and Suar, D. (2004) 'A Scale to Assess Ethical Leadership of Indian Private and Public Sector Managers', *Journal of Business Ethics* 49 (1): 13–26.

Kohlberg, L. (1976) 'Moral Stages and Moralization: The Cognitive Development Approach' in Lickona, T. (ed.) *Moral Development and Behaviour: Theory, Research and Social Issues.* New York: Holt, Rinehart and Winston, pp. 31–53.

Lasthuizen, K.M. (2008) *Leading to Integrity: Empirical Research into the Effects of Leadership on Ethics and Integrity*. Enschede, the Netherlands: Printpartners Ipskamp.

Lewis, C.W. (1991) *The Ethics Challenge in Public Service: A Problem Solving Guide*. San Francisco, CA: Jossey-Bass.

Mayer, D.M., Kuenzi, M., Greenbaum, R., Bardes, M. and Salvador, R. (2009) 'How Low Does Ethical Leadership Flow? Test of a Trickle-down Model', *Organizational Behavior and Human Decision Processes* 108 (1): 1–13.

McCall, J.J. (2002) 'Leadership and Ethics: Corporate Accountability to Whom, for What and by What Means?' *Journal of Business Ethics* 38 (1/2): 133–9.

Menzel, D.C. (2007) *Ethics Management for Public Administrators: Building Organizations of Integrity*. Armonk, NY and London: M.E. Sharpe.

—— (2009) *Ethics Moments in Government: Cases and Controversies*. Boca Raton, FL: CRC Press.

Michie, S. and Gooty, J. (2005) 'Values, Emotions, and Authenticity: Will the Real Leader Please Stand Up?' *Leadership Quarterly* 16 (3): 441–57.

Neubert, M.J., Carlson, D.S., Kacmar, K.M., Roberts, J.A. and Chonko, L.B. (2009) 'The Virtuous Influence of Ethical Leadership Behavior: Evidence from the Field', *Journal of Business Ethics* 90 (2): 157–70.

Paine, L.S. (1994) 'Managing for Organizational Integrity', *Harvard Business Review* 72 (2): 106–17.

Palanski, M.E. and Yammarino, F.J. (2009) 'Integrity and Leadership: A Multi-level Conceptual Framework', *The Leadership Quarterly* 20 (3): 405–20.

Parry, K.W. and Proctor-Thomson, S.B. (2002) 'Perceived Integrity of Transformational Leaders in Organisational Settings', *Journal of Business Ethics* 35 (2): 75–96.

Piccolo, R.F., Greenbaum, R., Den Hartog, D.N. and Folger, R. (2010) 'The Relationship Between Ethical Leadership and Core Job Characteristics', *Journal of Organizational Behavior* 31 (2–3): 259–78.

Resick, C.J., Hanges, P.J., Dickson, M.W. and Mitchelson, J.K. (2006) 'A Cross-cultural Examination of the Endorsement of Ethical Leadership', *Journal of Business Ethics* 63 (4): 345–59.

Roberts, R. (2009) 'The Rise of Compliance-based Ethics Management: Implications for Organizational Ethics', *Public Integrity* 11 (3): 261–77.

Simons, T.L. (1999) 'Behavioral Integrity as a Critical Ingredient for Transformational Leadership', *Journal of Organizational Change Management* 12 (2): 89–104.

Treviño, L.K. (1986) 'Ethical Decision Making in Organizations: A Person-Situation Interactionist Model', *Academy of Management Review* 11 (3): 601–17.

—— (1992) 'The Social Effects of Punishment in Organizations: A Justice Perspective', *Academy of Management Review* 17 (4): 647–76.

Treviño, L.K. and Brown, M.E. (2005). 'The Role of Leaders in Influencing Unethical Behavior in the Workplace', in Kidwell, R.E. Jr. and Martin, C.L. (eds) *Managing*

Organizational Deviance. Thousand Oaks, CA, London and New Delhi: Sage Publications, pp. 69–96.

Treviño, L.K., Brown, M.E. and Hartman, L.P. (2003) 'A Qualitative Investigation of Perceived Executive Ethical Leadership: Perceptions from Inside and Outside the Executive Suite', *Human Relations* 56 (1): 5–37.

Treviño, L.K., Hartman, L.P. and Brown, M.E. (2000) 'Moral Person and Moral Manager: How Executives Develop a Reputation for Ethical Leadership', *California Management Review* 42 (4): 128–42.

Treviño, L.K., Weaver, G.R., Gibson, D.G. and Toffler, B.L. (1999) 'Managing Ethics and Legal Compliance: What Works and What Hurts', *California Management Review* 41 (2): 131–51.

Turner, N., Barling, J., Epitropaki, O., Butcher, V. and Milner, C. (2002) 'Transformational Leadership and Moral Reasoning', *Journal of Applied Psychology* 87 (2): 304–11.

Van den Akker, L., Heres, L., Six, F.E. and Lasthuizen, K. (2009) 'Ethical Leadership and Trust: It's All About Meeting Expectations', *International Journal of Leadership and Organizational Studies* 5 (2): 102–22.

Van Wart, M. (2005) *Dynamics of Leadership in Public Service: Theory and Practice*. New York, London: M.E. Sharpe.

—— (2006) 'An Ethics-based Approach to Leadership' in West, J.P. and Berman, E.M. (eds) *The Ethics Edge*. 2nd edition. Washington, DC: ICMA Press, pp. 39–45.

Walumbwa, F.O., Mayer, D.M., Wang, P., Wang, H., Workman, K. and Christensen, A.L. (2011) 'Linking Ethical Leadership to Employee Performance: The Roles of Leader-Member Exchange, Self-efficacy, and Organizational Identification', *Organizational Behavior and Human Decision Processes* 115 (2): 204-213.

Weaver, G.R., Treviño, L.K. and Agle, B. (2005) '"Somebody I Look Up To": Ethical Role Models in Organizations', *Organizational Dynamics* 34 (4): 313–30.

Wittmer, D. (1992) 'Ethical Sensitivity and Managerial Decision-making: An Experiment', *Journal of Public Administration Research and Theory* 2 (4): 443–62.

Chapter 10

Conclusion

LEARNING OBJECTIVES

By the end of this chapter you should:

■ understand the changing context of public service ethics
■ recognize the impact of that changing context on public service values
■ reassert the relevance and importance of public service ethics.

KEY POINTS IN THIS CHAPTER

■ The public realm is where discussions of the public interest and public service ethics should be located, and yet this realm is in danger of turning into a theatre of private interests.
■ The changing context of public service delivery means that the notion of acting in the public interest is contested.
■ Despite many examples of the ethical failings of our leaders, a public ethos remains amongst the majority of both our officials and our citizens, expressed through the outrage that accompanies our frustrations with our leaders.

INTRODUCTION

Throughout this book we have analyzed the roles of public officials, looked at their organizational contexts and we have raised questions about the extent to which ethical principles can be universalized across different countries. At this stage, then, it would seem a futile exercise to revisit the notion of a common discourse that might characterize public service ethics. And yet, the notion of acting in the public interest is a constant feature that distinguishes public life from other activities. We recognize that the concept is contested and will be decided in different ways in different regimes – however, it is an enduring theme.

We also suggest that, irrespective of what ethical frameworks we draw upon, our relationships with others is at the heart of both ethics and the role of a public official. Those relationships need be governed by civility, respect, tolerance and empathy.

If we accept that there are enduring themes of public service ethics, we also need to recognize the changing context of the public realm and public service delivery.

THE CHANGING LANDSCAPE OF PUBLIC SERVICES

> In general, one can argue that the public sector's responsibility for affecting the public interest is compromised and limited by the use of networks.
>
> (Agranoff and McGuire 2001: 310)

Delivering public services through different organizations working together is now commonplace. It is usual to find public, private and third-sector organizations sharing in the production of economic development, health and social care, or environmental sustainability. Much has been written on the reasons for such close working relationships (Head 2008), what forms they might take (Klijn 2008), how they are managed or how effective they are (Mandell and Keast 2008; Skelcher and Sullivan 2008). Whatever form they take – whether partnerships or loose networks, sharing goals and values and building trust – all are considered to be key ingredients in their success. In the wealth of research that has been undertaken in the last 20 years we find that the impact on the values of public officials who have engaged with partners from different sectors has been under-examined. This changing context of public service delivery will impact the motivation of public officials as they are exposed to different value sets.

Partnerships and networks are dynamic, often lack coherence and involve competing sets of values. They involve not just individual motivations but expectations of the behaviour of others (Koppenjan 2008). Motivation, in this sense, then cannot be isolated from relationships with others. Relations are typically horizontal in such networks, rather than vertical, and the concept of 'making a difference' is not clear-cut in a world of contested performance outcomes.

There are different types of relationships, from co-operation, co-ordination to collaboration. In one sense the three types can be mapped onto a continuum from loose to close-knit ties, with the supposition that the closer one gets to collaboration the more sharing is involved. As Thomson, Perry and Miller (2007: 25) describe it:

> Collaboration is a process in which autonomous or semi-autonomous actors interact through formal or informal negotiation, jointly creating rules and structures governing their relationships and ways to act or decide on the issues that brought them together; it is a process involving shared norms and mutually beneficial interactions.

Different intensities will require different stages of relationship-building, and motivation may change over time depending on the development of the network/partnership.

> [I]t is not the formal requirements that keeps a network together, but, rather the ability to build mutual goodwill and commitment among the participants.
>   (Mandell and Keast 2008: 721)

And yet Frederickson (2007: 291) poses the question:

> When will people sing an anthem to a contractor, wear the uniform of a network, or pledge allegiance to non-jurisdictional forms of governance? Probably not soon.

THE PUBLIC REALM

Whenever personal disputes between individuals come to dominate public debate then the public realm is diminished. Witness the last years of the Blair/Brown era in UK politics, when the deteriorating personal relationship between Prime Minister Tony Blair and his Chancellor of the Exchequer, Gordon Brown, had disastrous consequences for the Labour Party and for the government as a whole. Currently, in Australia, a country that has managed to escape much of the worst of the global financial crises, public debate is dominated by possible leadership challenges within the ruling party itself, as supporters of both former PM Kevin Rudd and the current PM (February 2012), Julia Gillard, re-open old sores and find new ways of point scoring. In the meantime, sitting in the wings, is Opposition Leader Tony Abbott whose main strategy focuses on highlighting the weaknesses of the above two rather than developing a vision for Australia for the next decade. We could speculate that political debate ought to be dominated by concerns with the environment, commitments to future generations and dealing with the consequences of economic, social and political failure. We might also speculate that, in the case of Australia, the successes of the management of the economy and lessons for, and challenges of, the future, particularly in the 'Asian Century' might provide a focus for more informed political debate.

We have discussed the importance of ethical leadership, and in times of economic crises we need to trust our political leaders and be confident that they are acting in the public interest rather than pursuing personal or narrow sectional interests. The phrase 'we are all in this together', used by current British Prime Minister David Cameron, is difficult to swallow when city and bankers' bonuses are returning to levels last achieved before the global financial crisis, a crisis many believe was caused, in part, by the excesses of the financial institutions. As Adam Smith [1759] (1976) worded it over 250 years ago:

> The disposition to admire, and almost to worship, the rich and the powerful, and to despise, or, at least, to neglect, persons of poor and mean condition [is] the great and most universal cause of the corruption of our moral sentiments.
>
> (Chap III, para 1: 61)

And yet, all is not lost: in other countries individuals are standing up to be counted in the fight to enhance accountability in the public realm. In India, a popular Indian yoga guru, Baba Ramdev, carried out a much-publicized hunger strike aimed at pressuring the government to take action against corruption. The yoga guru's protest campaign is part of a public push to demand government accountability for several corruption scandals, including the sale of mobile phone licences at below-market rates, which is said to have cost the government up to 40 billion US dollars. The campaign has received worldwide coverage. Perhaps less publicized, in Brazil, President Dilma Roussef has introduced legislation towards greater transparency and accountability.

Clearly values in society do change and develop in unforeseen ways and what counts as acceptable behaviour in one country and at one time may be considered unacceptable in different countries and at different times. What are we to make of recent claims in the UK that senior public officials were being paid through private companies that they had set up to avoid being taxed at source? Treasury Chief Secretary Danny Alexander and Cabinet Office Minister Francis Maude have written to all government departments asking them to examine their reward structures as part of a clampdown on excessive bonuses. On 15 February 2012 *The Guardian* reported that the salaries of more than 25 senior staff at the Department of Health are paid direct to limited companies. In some cases, the newspaper claimed, individuals are being paid more than £250,000 a year, plus expenses. The payments total more than £4 million in one year. The department apologized for any 'misunderstanding' after previously specifying that none of its civil servants were paid through limited companies. One Whitehall source said: 'We cannot defend these arrangements, but it maybe it is very common in Whitehall and this is just the tip of an iceberg.'

Given our comments above concerning city and bankers' bonuses, should we be surprised at these public officials? Perhaps the post-modern condition that we discussed in Chapter 2 makes it easier to understand, if not to condone, the apparently self-interested actions of those whom we trust to act in the public interest.

And yet, as we discussed in Chapter 4, individuals are motivated to act in the public interest and we should not accept the impoverishment of political debate by populist politicians. It is a cliché that ethics is not a spectator sport but does require the courage to make unpopular decisions or to stand up against unethical practices both within and outside of our public services. Not just courage; moreover, the underrated virtue of persistence to pursue ethical courses of action when it might be easier to let it go.

As John Gray (2009: 43) has argued:

> In practical life, seeking compromise among irreconcilable aims is a mark of wisdom. In intellectual life, it is a sign of confusion.

We have argued throughout for just such a practical approach to ethics; for a balanced approach that does not side with a framework that is neither compliance-driven nor integrity-focused alone. We have recognized the need to balance individual, organizational and societal values. We have also suggested that there is something distinctive about working in and for the public services, and which has motivated generations of public officials. As the public domain becomes even more and more blurred it comes into contact with private and group interests, so that clarity in understanding the public interest is crucial. Ultimately we want to know if public service ethics are improving and if so, what causes that improvement, and why. We still have a long way to go to identify causal factors, if indeed such an enterprise is worthwhile. Thus, our concern has been with the practice of ethics, drawing upon those theories that might help us in our deliberations.

REFERENCES

Agranoff, R. and McGuire, M. (2001) 'Big Questions in Public Network Management', *Journal of Public Administration Research and Theory* 11 (3): 295–326.

Frederickson, H.G. (2007) 'Whatever Happened to Public Administration? Governance, Governance Everywhere' in Ferlie, E., Lynn, L.E. Jr. and Pollitt, C. (eds) *The Oxford Handbook of Public Management*. Oxford: Oxford University Press, pp. 282–304.

Gray, J. (2009) *Gray's Anatomy: Selected Writings*. London: Penguin.

Head, B.W. (2008) 'Assessing Network-based Collaborations: Effectiveness for Whom?' *Public Management Review* 10 (6): 733–49.

Klijn, E.H. (2008) 'Governance and Governance Networks in Europe', *Public Management Review* 10 (4): 505–25.

Koppenjan, J. (2008) 'Creating a Playing Field for Assessing the Perfection of Network Collaboration by Performance Measures', *Public Management Review* 10 (6): 699–714.

Mandell, M.P. and Keast, R. (2008) 'Evaluating the Effectiveness on Inter-organizational Relations Through Networks', *Public Management Review* 10 (6): 715–35.

Skelcher, C. and Sullivan, H. (2008) 'Theory-driven Approaches to Analysing Collaborative Performance', *Public Management Review* 10 (6): 751–71.

Smith, A. [1759] (1976) *The Theory of Moral Sentiments*. Oxford: Clarendon Press.

Thomson, A.M., Perry, J.L. and Miller, T.K. (2007) 'Conceptualisng and Measuring Collaboration', *Journal of Public Administration Research and Theory* 19 (1): 23–56.

Index

Page numbers in *Italics* represent Tables

New eBook Library Collection

Taylor & Francis **eBooks**
Taylor & Francis Group

eFocus on Routledge/ECPR Studies in European Political Science

30 day free trials available!

The Routledge/ECPR Studies in European Political Science series is published in association with the European Consortium for Political Research - the leading organisation concerned with the growth and development of political science in Europe.

The series presents high-quality edited volumes on topics at the leading edge of current interest in political science and related fields, with contributions from leading European scholars.

The Series Editor is **Thomas Poguntke**, Ruhr-Universität Bochum, Germany.

Now for the first time, this series is available as a comprehensive eCollection comprising 69 eBooks.

Key titles in the collection include:

- *Social Capital and European Democracy*, edited by **Marco Maraffi**, University of Milano, Italy; **Kenneth Newton**, University of Southampton, UK; **Jan Van Deth**, University of Mannheim, Germany; and **Paul Whitely**, University of Essex, UK.

- *Politicians, Bureaucrats and Administrative Reform*, edited by **B. Guy Peters**, University of Pittsburgh, USA; and **Jon Pierre**, Gothenburg University, Sweden.

- *The Territorial Politics of Welfare*, edited by **Nicola McEwen**, University of Edinburgh, UK; and **Luis Moreno**, Spanish National Research Council (CSIC), Madrid, Spain.

The **European Consortium for Political Research (ECPR)** is an independent scholarly association of 350 institutional members, supporting and encouraging training, research and cross-national co-operation of many thousands of academics and graduate students specializing in political science and all its sub-disciplines.

eFocus on ECPR is available as a subscription package of 69 titles with 5 new eBooks per annum.

Recommend this package to your librarian today!

Order now for guaranteed capped price increase.

For a complete list of titles, visit:
www.ebooksubscriptions.com/eFocusECPR
www.ebooksubscriptions.com

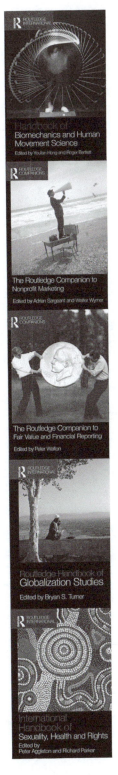